Collins

11+
Non-Verbal Reasoning

Complete Revision, Practice & Assessment

For the CEM test

Introduction

11+ Tests and Non-Verbal Reasoning

CEM (The Centre for Evaluation and Monitoring) is one of the two major bodies responsible for setting 11+ tests. The CEM exam usually consists of two papers and in each paper pupils are tested on their skills in verbal, non-verbal and numerical reasoning. Exams are separated into short, timed sections delivered by audio instructions.

It appears the content required for CEM exams changes from year to year, and the level at which pupils are tested ranges from county to county. Before sitting the exam, your child should be well prepared, with solid foundations built in the three core skills.

Non-verbal reasoning tests help to assess a child's potential to work successfully with abstract concepts and solve spatial reasoning problems, independent of language. The results are good indicators of future learning and success in a number of subject areas.

It is particularly important to provide non-verbal reasoning practice as your child may not have come across these types of question before. The questions feature shapes, pictures and patterns and allow children to demonstrate their ability to analyse, deduce and infer from close observation.

About this Book

This book is split into three sections to help children to prepare for the non-verbal reasoning components of the CEM test. Features of each section include:

Revision
- Easy-to-digest revision notes for each topic.
- Develops the skills needed to answer test questions.
- 'Remember' boxes to emphasise key points and provide tips.
- Quick Tests to check understanding of a topic before moving on.

Practice
- Topic-based questions to practise the skills.
- Increases familiarity with the questions expected in the test.
- Tests are timed to develop the ability to work at speed.

Assessment
- Six assessment papers offer multiple opportunities to have a go at a test and gradually improve performance.
- Familiarises your child with the format of the papers.
- Enables your child to practise working at speed and with accuracy.

Answers and explanations are provided at the back of the book to help you mark your child's answers and support their preparation.

Progress charts are also included to help you record scores on the practice tests and assessment papers.

ebook

To access the ebook visit collins.co.uk/ebooks and follow the step-by-step instructions.

The Assessment Papers

Spend some time talking with your child so that they understand the purpose of the assessment papers and how doing them will help them to prepare for the actual exam.

Agree with your child a good time to take the assessment papers. This should be when they are fresh and alert. You also need to find a good place to work, a place that is comfortable and free from distractions. Being able to see a clock is helpful as they learn how to pace themselves.

Explain how they may find some parts easy and others more challenging, but that they need to have a go at every question. If they 'get stuck' on a question, they should just mark it with an asterisk and carry on. At the end of a section, they may have time to go back and try again.

As in the actual exam, the answers for the assessment papers should not be written on the question booklet. They should be marked on the separate answer sheet (as in the real test a computer will be used in the marking process). Answers should be carefully marked in pencil with a straight line on the answer sheet in pencil.

Answer sheets for the practice tests and assessment papers can be found at the very back of the book, on pages 153–160. Further copies of these answer sheets can be downloaded from **collins.co.uk/11plus**.

How much time should be given?

The time allowed is given on the introductory pages at the beginning of each section. These timings are based on the challenging time allocations that would be expected in the actual 11+ test. CEM tests are designed to be time pressured and you don't necessarily need to complete all the questions to pass or do well.

If your child has not finished after the allocated time, ask them to draw a line to indicate where they are on the test at that time, and allow them to finish. This allows them to practise every question type, as well as allowing you to get a score showing how many were correctly answered in the time available. It will also help you and your child to think about ways to increase speed of working if this is an area that your child finds difficult. If your child completes a section in less than the allocated minutes, encourage them to go through and check their answers carefully.

Marking

Award one mark for each correct answer. Half marks are not allowed. No marks are deducted for wrong answers.

If scores are low, look at the paper and identify which question types seem to be harder for your child. Then spend some time going over them together. If your child is very accurate and gets correct answers, but works too slowly, try getting them to do the test sections with time targets going through. If you are helpful and look for ways to help your child, they will grow in confidence and feel well prepared when they take the actual exam.

Please note: As the content varies from year to year and county to county in CEM exams, a good score in the assessment papers of this book does not guarantee a pass. Likewise, a lower score may not necessarily suggest a fail.

Acknowledgements

The authors and publisher are grateful to the copyright holders for permission to use quoted materials and images.

All images are © Shutterstock.com and © HarperCollins*Publishers* Ltd

Every effort has been made to trace copyright holders and obtain their permission for the use of copyright material. The authors and publisher will gladly receive information enabling them to rectify any error or omission in subsequent editions. All facts are correct at time of going to press.

Published by Collins
An imprint of HarperCollins*Publishers*
1 London Bridge Street
London SE1 9GF

ISBN: 978-0-00-839891-0

First published 2020

10 9 8 7 6 5 4 3 2 1

© HarperCollins*Publishers* Ltd. 2020

British Library Cataloguing in Publication Data.

A CIP record of this book is available from the British Library.

Publishers: Clare Souza and Katie Sergeant
Contributing authors: Beatrix Woodhead, Neil R Williams, Val Mitchell, Sally Moon and Faisal Nasim
Project Management and Development: Richard Toms and Rebecca Skinner
Cover Design: Kevin Robbins and Sarah Duxbury
Inside Concept Design and Page Layout: Ian Wrigley
Production: Karen Nulty
Printed in the United Kingdom

MIX
Paper from
responsible source
FSC® C007454

This book is produced from independently certified FSC™ paper to ensure responsible forest management.

For more information visit: www.harpercollins.co.uk/green

Contents

Revision

Practice

Assessment

Answers

Making Connections

You should be able to:

- recognise the most common connections between a series of shapes
- identify similarities and differences between a series of shapes
- spot distractions in order to eliminate irrelevant connections.

What to Expect

- There are lots of small ways that images can be changed.
- In questions that require you to make connections, you will see a wide range of similarities including shape size, shading, the number of shapes, position, the variety of shapes and angles.
- In making connections, you will need to look at each type of connection individually.
- When you combine two or more connections, you start to build relationships between the shapes.
- Sometimes questions will show a connection that doesn't quite seem to fit. These are known as 'distractions'. They are there to make the questions a little bit harder.

Skills in Understanding Connections

- A connection is something that is similar about the images you are looking at. You can use connections to compare the images.
- Spotting the connections is an important skill, but being able to spot what changes is equally important. Putting the connections and the changes together will lead you to the answer.

Example

The first shape is a black triangle and the second shape is a black circle. Both shapes are regular.

The shading is clearly a connection between the two images. If you were looking at a question that asked you to pick a shape that could be grouped with these two, you would be looking for a shape that was black.

Note also that both shapes are regular. This is useful information, especially if there are two black shapes to pick from.

In this example, you can see that the shape of the figure is the only thing that changes.

Remember

Regular shapes have angles of the same size and sides of the same length.

Squares and equilateral triangles are two examples of regular shapes. A circle is also a regular shape, despite not having any straight sides.

Remember

Irregular shapes have different sized angles or sides of different length. A rectangle is irregular as not all the sides are the same length, despite all the angles being the same size.

Question Type Skills

- Non-verbal reasoning questions are best approached one step at a time. Look for anything that seems to remain the same and anything that seems to change consistently.
- In 'odd one out' questions, you could be shown five images and asked to pick the one that doesn't really belong with the others.
- In 'most like' questions, you could be shown two or three images that are part of a 'set'. You might then be asked to pick one from a group of five or six that should also be part of the set.

Common Connections

Line Style Connections

- Solid lines are the most common type of line you will see. Generally, any shape that isn't white will have a solid line as it would be too difficult to spot the pattern in the line against the shading of the shape. The lines could be of different thicknesses.
- Dashed lines could appear on the outline of shapes or on arrows, but these could have different patterns.

Shape Connections

- Regular shapes look more familiar and this can make them easier to compare, even though the connections are generally the same as those for irregular shapes.

Example
What connections can you find between these two shapes?

Both shapes have dashed lines around the outside and the dashes are the same length. They have no shading on the inside. They are both regular shapes: one is a square and the other is a pentagon.

- Irregular shapes can be trickier than regular shapes as they are less familiar.
- A set of irregular shapes may have the same number of corners or the same number of straight sides.

Example
Can you see any connections between these two shapes?

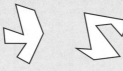

Both shapes have solid lines around the outside and have no shading on the inside. They both have nine sides and corners.

Shading Connections

- Since colour is not used, different levels of solid shading are likely to be used on the shapes in the test.
- This shading could be black, dark grey, light grey or white (i.e. no shading). Patterned shading, such as stripes, may also be seen in shapes.

Size Connections

- Another possible change that can occur between shapes is size.
- The figures can be made bigger or smaller but stay the same shape, just like the two circles shown to the right.
- You are more likely to see this sort of change in a regular shape than in an irregular one.

Arrow Connections

- Wherever arrows are used in questions, there are a couple of things that can be changed.
- The first is the design of the arrowhead.

> **Example**
> Look at the four arrows and see how the arrowheads have changed.
>
>
>
> One is a simple triangle, one is just two lines forming a 'V', the third is a triangle with a curved base and the last is a diamond.

Remember

Arrows can point in various directions, so some of the arrowheads may look different because the arrows are shown at an angle.

- The tail of the arrow can be another important connection.

> **Example**
> Look at these three arrows with identical heads.
>
>
>
> Each arrow has a different number of tail 'fins'. The first has one, the second has two and the third has three. You should count each pair of lines as one fin.

- Generally the fins will point in the same direction as the head.
- Arrows can also point in a range of directions. They can point up, down, left or right. They can also point diagonally towards any corner of a box.

Remember

Direction is not the same as rotation. When you talk about 'direction', you are looking for arrows or shapes that point in the same direction. When you talk about 'rotation', you are looking for a repeating degree of turn across a series of boxes.

Shape and Line Connections

- Another common feature in questions is a 'dumbbell' consisting of a line with shapes at each end.
- Look at the following dumbbell shapes and how the symmetrical shapes have changed:

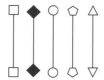

- The shapes at either end of each line are symmetrical. Here there are squares, circles, pentagons and triangles.
- Often the shapes are both shaded or patterned in the same way.
- Some lines can have the same shape at each end of the line but arranged asymmetrically:

- Sometimes the shapes will be positioned symmetrically but will have different shading or patterns:

Angle Connections

- Sometimes you can look at a question and struggle to spot an angle connection, as it is not something you will generally think about. Shading is much more obvious as it is more visual.
- The connection might be that all the shapes have a right angle or an obtuse angle. It could also be that the angles with a connection are acute.
- Looking at the shapes below, at first glance they might just seem to be triangles. However, on closer inspection, one has acute angles only, one has a right angle and one has an obtuse angle.

- Spotting right angles can be tricky if the lines making the right angle are not horizontal and vertical, as that is what you are used to looking for. If you suspect that an angle is a right angle, make one of the lines horizontal either by angling your head or turning the paper. If the other line is vertical then you know you have got a right angle.

Revision

> **Remember**
>
> Shapes positioned at either end of a line do not have to be symmetrical, so pay attention to how they are positioned relative to the line.

> **Remember**
>
> When you look at angles, it may help to remember the following:
>
> | | |
> |---|---|
> | An acute angle is less than 90°. | |
> | A right angle is exactly 90°. | |
> | An obtuse angle is between 90° and 180°. | |
> | A reflex angle is more than 180°. | |

Symmetry Connections

- Shapes may 'share' a line of symmetry or have their own line of symmetry.
- The isosceles triangle shown on the right has one (vertical) line of symmetry.
- In some questions each box may contain a number of shapes and a line of symmetry will go 'through' the box.
- Look at this box containing four shapes and a horizontal line of symmetry:

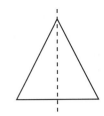

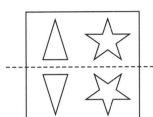

- Sometimes a series of shapes can be connected by sharing rotational symmetry. For example, the shapes below all have rotational symmetry order 2, which means that they will fit inside their own outline twice if rotated:

Quick Test

1. Look at the five shapes in each row. What connects four of the shapes and makes the other shape the odd one out? Find the shape that is most unlike the others.

a)

   A   B   C   D   E

b)

   A   B   C   D   E

2. The two shapes on the left are part of a set. Which of the five shapes on the right belongs with the set?

a)

               A   B   C   D   E

b)

               A   B   C   D   E

Finding Similarities and Differences

- You could be required to make connections between single shapes or between groups of shapes.
- Most connections will be relevant, but others may not be.

Single Shapes

- Questions using single shapes are usually the easiest as there are only a few possible connections.

> **Example**
> Look at these two single shapes. Find the similarities and differences between them.
>
>
>
> **Similarities**:
> - Both shapes have four sides.
> - Both shapes have solid lines.
> - Both shapes are white (i.e. unshaded).
>
> **Differences**:
> - The first shape is a diamond, the second is a square.
> - The angles in the first shape are different to those in the second.

> **Remember**
>
> Even if a connection seems very obvious, do not rule it out because you think it might be 'too simple'.

Small Groups of Simple Shapes

- Small groups of simple shapes may have connections in common.

> **Example**
> Look at these two groups of shapes. Find the similarities and differences between them.
>
>
>
> **Similarities**:
> - Both boxes have four shapes.
> - Both boxes have two triangles.
> - Both boxes have a quadrilateral.
> - All the shapes are white (unshaded) with solid lines.
>
> **Differences**:
> - There are a total of 15 corners in the shapes in the first box, but 16 in the second box.
> - The first box has shapes with a total of five right angles, but there are none in the second box.
> - Unlike the first box, all the shapes in the second box are symmetrical.
> - There is a pentagon in the first box and a hexagon in the second box.
>
> If you had to find a similar group of shapes to the two shown above, you might be looking for a box with two triangles, a quadrilateral and one more shape, all of which were white.

Segmented Shapes

- Segmented shapes are usually regular shapes that have been split into various pieces or sections. They will often be connected by shading.

Example
Look at these two single shapes. Find the similarities and differences between them.

Similarities:
- Both shapes are split into eight equal segments.
- The lines for the segments seem to be in the same place.
- Each shape has two segments shaded black.
- Each shape has one segment which has vertical lines.

Differences:
- In the first shape the shaded sections are all separate, but in the second shape they are all together.

Compound Shapes

- Compound shapes are made up of several smaller shapes and often look like something you would recognise.
- The compound shape shown to the right looks like a rather old car.
- Compound shapes can have lots of connections as the smaller shapes can have similarities of their own.
- For more on compound shapes, see pages 26–27.

Spotting Distractions

- Not every connection is relevant to the problem. Sometimes you will find that connections have been put in as a distraction.
- The distraction might be extra shapes, compound shapes, the type of shading, the combination of the shapes, the arrows or another kind of feature.

Example
The two images on the left are part of a set. Which of the five images on the right belongs with the set?

  |
                       A   B   C   D   E

What is similar and what is different about the two boxes on the left?

Similarities:
- They both have one hexagon in them.
- All of the shapes have solid lines and no shading.
- The shapes in both boxes have a total of 16 corners.

Differences:

- The first box has two shapes; the second one has three shapes.

The combination of shapes in the box is not going to be relevant, but the hexagon or the number of corners will be.

Hexagon: Options B, C and E have at least one hexagon in them.

Corners: Option A has 16 corners, B has 6, C has 15, D has 15 and E has 12.

Both B and E have one hexagon, but the number of corners is different. If the hexagon and just straight lines are the deciding factors, it could be E. If the number of corners is important, the answer has to be A.

In this example the answer is **A**. The hexagon was the distraction in this question.

Quick Test

1. The two images on the left are part of a set. Which of the five images on the right belongs with the set?

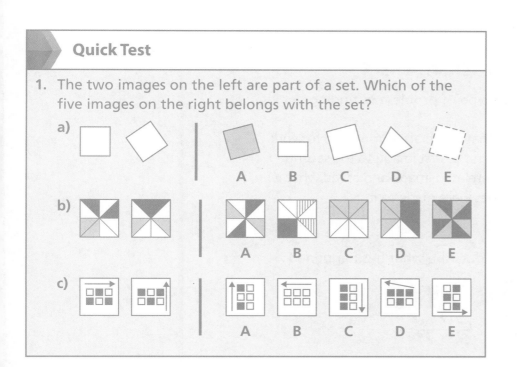

Finding Relationships

You should be able to:

- spot different relationships
- recognise the three different types of reflection
- work with rotated shapes
- apply relationships linking one pair of shapes to a third shape.

What to Expect

- Finding relationships is all about spotting how images are linked together.
- The key to understanding these questions is to look at what is going on from one image to the next. For example:

- When finding relationships, you could see changes in the following: shape; size; shading; the number of shapes; the position of shapes; the variety of shapes; angles.
- These changes will often be combined with each other or with new connections – such as rotation and reflection – to create a relationship.
- Some new connections can involve jigsaw-like pieces and how they fit together. In some questions they will line up so that it is fairly obvious how they fit. In other questions they will be the wrong way round so that it is not that clear how they fit together.
- Irregular shapes will be used more often. These are shapes where the angles are not all the same size as each other, and the sides are different lengths.

Skills in Spotting Relationships

- 'Pairs questions' are a common type of problem in finding relationships.
- You could be shown two images that are related. You need to work out what has happened to get from the first image to the second one. You will then be shown an unrelated image and asked what it would look like if the same changes were made to it.

> **Example**
> Look at these two images and describe what has happened.
>
>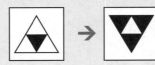

Shading: the shapes have swapped their shading.

Reflection: the whole image has been reflected in a horizontal mirror line.

Now that you know what has happened to these two images, you can work out what the boat image shown right will look like if the same changes are made to it.

What 'connections' do you need to make?

The first step is to swap the shading – what was black in the first box should become white in the second box and what was white in the first box should become black in the second box.

The second step is to reflect the complete image in a horizontal mirror line.

Relationships with More Connections

Example

Look at the two boxes below. How many connections go together to make up this relationship?

- The circle gets smaller.
- The circle changes from black to white.
- The trapezium gets bigger.
- The trapezium changes from white to black.
- Both shapes appear to rotate 90° anti-clockwise around the box.

There are five connections making up the relationship.

Now try to make the relationship a little more general.

- The two shapes swap their shading.
- The two shapes swap their approximate size.
- The whole box rotates 90° anti-clockwise about the middle of the box.

Now try to apply this relationship to this new image:

What 'connections' do you need to make?

How will the connections change this image?

- The larger shape should get smaller – that is the hexagon in this example.
- The smaller shape should get bigger.
- The black shape should become white.
- The white shape should become black.
- Both shapes should rotate 90° anti-clockwise around the box.

Changes to Shape

- Here we will focus on how shapes can change from one box to another.
- When shapes change, there is a range of features that can alter, such as shape, size, shading, proportion and the combination of shapes.

The simplest change you will see is that a shape changes size, but stays in proportion.	
Shapes can be 'stretched' or 'squashed'. Often one side of a shape stays the same while the other sides change.	
The shading of a shape can be changed. The shading might be solid black, solid grey, solid white or patterned in some way.	

- In some questions the changes to the shapes are 'linked'.

Example
Look at these two boxes. They both contain squares, triangles and circles, but there are different numbers of each and they are all in different positions.

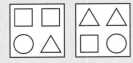

What are the similarities?
- The two identical shapes are on the top row.
- There are four shapes in each box.
- If you look more closely you can see that where the squares were, you now have triangles. Where the triangle was you now have a circle and where the circle was you now have a square. The shapes have all changed order.

- In some questions the shapes are the same, but you can see that the shading has changed.

Example
What changes have taken place between these two boxes?

- The shape that was black is now white.
- The shapes that were white are now striped.
- The shape that was striped is now black.

Proportion and Number

- Proportion questions will generally involve a number of identical shapes or large shapes broken up into a number of segments.

Example

Look at these two shapes. What proportion has been shaded in each one?

In the first shape every other segment is shaded, so you can say half of the shape is shaded.

In the second shape pairs of segments are shaded, but it is still half the shape that is shaded.

In both shapes half of the segments are shaded black.

Imagine you have to find a shape that will match these two shapes. What might it look like?

As long as four out of the eight segments are shaded, you have a match.

> **Remember**
>
> Square paper can be a useful tool for getting used to what different proportions look like. You can draw boxes and shade in different numbers of squares. Some squares might not be touching.

- Sometimes you will look at pictures of different shapes and wonder what the link between them is. The 'number' of something might be the last thing you will try once you have discounted all the other options.

- Something about the shapes in the boxes might have a constant number.

Example

What is it about the shapes in these two boxes that has a constant number?

At first glance the two boxes seem to have nothing in common.

The first box has two rectangles and two triangles. The second box has two pentagons and a rectangle.

The shading of all the shapes is the same but the number of shapes is different.

Even though both boxes have at least one rectangle, the rectangles are not the same size or in the same position.

Knowing that the number of shapes is different means you can rule out rotation and reflection.

If you count the number of corners the shapes have, you will find that there are 14 corners in total in both boxes.

Now you need to check each of the possible answers to see which of them also has 14 corners. Do check them all, even if the first seems to fit. If there is more than one answer option with the right number of corners, you might find that something else is also important.

- In some questions you will see numbers that increase or decrease in regular steps. These questions are covered in more detail in number patterns on pages 42–43.

> **Example**
> These boxes contain a series of shapes. No two boxes are the same and none of the shapes inside the boxes match each other.
>
>
>
> The first box has a rectangle; the second has two triangles; the third has a trapezium and a diamond; the last has two pentagons.
>
> If you look at the number of corners, you can see that the first box has four, the second has six, the third has eight, and the last has ten.
>
> The pattern is that the number of corners is going up by two each time.
>
> That means the next box will have 12 corners. The shapes could be two hexagons, or three quadrilaterals, or even four triangles, but there will be 12 corners.

Moving and Connecting Shapes

Shapes Moving Apart
- Questions may involve shapes moving around a box and possibly rotating at the same time.
- Sometimes you will see that one element from the image moves but the other elements remain the same.
- One of the simplest movements is when a shape moves from the inside to the outside of another shape.
- Usually the shapes that move will stay the same size and the same way up, as in this example:

- Sometimes a shape leaves a 'hole' behind when it moves. The square in the following box has moved from inside the circle to outside. The size of the shapes remains the same.

- Depending on how you think, you will either call it a hole or say another square has been added. As long as you can spot the connection, it doesn't matter how you think about it.

Remember

Many of the skills in connecting shapes are the same ones that you would use when doing a jigsaw puzzle. The difference is that the shapes are plain and there is no picture to help you – it is a bit like doing the puzzle with all the pieces turned over.

Shapes Joining Together

- The simplest form of bringing regular shapes together is when one shape moves to the inside of another shape.
- You might see one shape that is significantly bigger than the others and the smaller shapes move inside it.

Example

How have the regular shapes in these two boxes been joined?

The triangle and the circle have moved inside the rectangle.

Watch out for changes in the positions of the shapes, as in this example – if the shapes swap sides, it is likely to be important to the answer.

- Sometimes it may seem that shapes join together to make a new shape.
- Shown on the right are four triangles joined together at the corners so it looks like a square has been added.
- If you take away each triangle in turn, the lines that make the square will disappear as well.

- Some shapes, especially identical shapes, can join together along their sides to make a pattern that fits closely together (tessellates). Consider how the triangles shown on the right have been joined.
- Irregular shapes will often look like jigsaw pieces with bits that stick out of one piece and fit into another.

- Will the two irregular shapes shown on the right join together? Like most jigsaw pieces, these shapes will join up to make a more recognisable shape – a rectangle in this case.
- You will not always be shown the shapes so that they line up. You may have to rotate them before you can join them together.
- The questions may try to trip you up by swapping the shading when the pieces are joined together or by turning the pieces upside down.

Combining Shapes

- Another form of joining shapes together is when one shape is placed on top of another to form a new figure.
- When this happens, generally you will need to imagine the shapes are on a clear background, as if you have drawn one on tracing paper and put it on top of the other.

> **Remember**
>
> Questions will often involve more than one relationship.

Example

Look at the first two shapes. How have they been combined to make the third figure?

 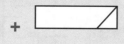

The first two shapes have been laid on top of one another and the second shape has been rotated. Notice how the shapes have not changed size at all when combined.

- Sometimes, you may need to imagine what a figure will look like with one part taken away:

- Just as before, the shapes here have not changed size at all when they are separated. You can imagine the lines in the second shape being removed one at a time from the first figure.
- Once you think you have the answer, you can check by imagining overlapping the two separate component parts to see if they would make the original figure.

Quick Test

1. The two boxes on the left are a pair. Work out which of the five boxes on the right completes the second pair in the same way as the first pair.

   a)

   A   B   C   D   E

   b)

   A   B   C   D   E

2. There are two similar boxes on the left. Work out which of the five boxes on the right is most like the first two.

   a)

   A   B   C   D   E

   b)

   A   B   C   D   E

3. The two boxes on the left are a pair. Work out which of the five boxes on the right completes the second pair in the same way as the first pair.

   a)

   A   B   C   D   E

   b)

   A   B   C   D   E

Reflections in Vertical Lines

- Reflections are another type of relationship that are likely to appear in questions.
- The simplest reflection is that of a single shape.
- Look at this triangle, which is pointing to the right:

- Imagine that there is a vertical mirror line just beyond the point on the right-hand side.
- Each point has to travel to that imaginary line and then the same distance past it.
- Once the lines are joined up, you should get a triangle pointing to the left:

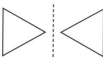

- When the shapes are in boxes, the vertical edges can be used as if they are mirror lines.
- A second type of reflection in a vertical line involves shading.
- This overall shape is an equilateral triangle that is pointing up. If it didn't have any shading, the reflection would be the same as the original shape:

- Once again, imagine a vertical mirror line just to the right of the triangle.
- Each point has to travel to that line and the same distance past it, and that includes the point on the base where the edge of the shading is:

- A third type of reflection in a vertical line involves more than one shape.
- Here you have an equilateral triangle with a square and a circle inside it:

- Put that imaginary vertical mirror line on the right-hand side again and reflect the triangle.
- You can reflect the square in the same way – you have got four corners to work with.
- You should find that the circle and the square seem to swap places inside the triangle:

Remember

Although you won't be shown a dotted mirror line, that doesn't mean you can't draw one in.

Remember

Each point on each shape will end up the same distance from the mirror line, but on the opposite side of the line.

- Look at the mirror line for the box reflected here:

Remember

Reflections in vertical lines can be seen as reflections in a big mirror, such as those you see on wardrobe doors. If you have a mirror like this at home, sit beside it and hold up various shapes to find out how they are reflected.

- Shapes that are not in the middle of the box can give you big clues about reflections as their position will move, just like the black circle in this example.
- For questions that are not in grids, you need to imagine that your mirror line is outside the box rather than going through the middle.

Reflections in Horizontal Lines

- With the exception of questions in grids, reflections in horizontal lines can be tricky to spot as the images are lined up across the page rather than down it.
- Look at this triangle. Imagine that there is a horizontal mirror line just below the shape:

- Each point has to travel to that imaginary line and then the same distance past it. Once the lines are joined up in this example, you get a triangle pointing down:

- When the shapes are in boxes, the horizontal edges can be used as if they are mirror lines.
- Reflections involving shading or more than one shape work in exactly the same way – only the direction has changed.

Reflections in Diagonal Lines

- Most reflections you encounter will be in horizontal or vertical lines. However, you may occasionally face a question with a diagonal reflection line at 45° to the base of the box (either inside it or outside it).
- Imagine that there is a mirror line going diagonally through the box below from top left to bottom right. Use a real mirror if this helps. You will need to turn it around to check the other side of the reflection.

- Each point has to travel the shortest distance possible to that imaginary line and then the same distance past it:

- The shapes will always remain the same, but their positions will change:

- If you find it easier to think about a rotation and a reflection being combined, then use that to help you work out the answer.
- Lots of people find that reflections in a diagonal line are confusing as the image seems to fold over itself.
- You can also break this skill down into two steps to make it easier.
- Start with the same image as above and reflect it in a line that goes from top left to bottom right:

- The first step is to rotate in the direction of the lowest point on the mirror line; as that is the bottom right you need to rotate 90° clockwise.
- The final step is to reflect the rotated shape in a vertical mirror line:

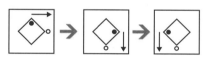

- As you can see, the final answer is the same as before.
- If the diagonal mirror line had been going from bottom left to top right, you would need to rotate the shape 90° anti-clockwise before reflecting it in a vertical mirror line:

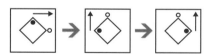

Rotations

- Rotations can occur clockwise or anti-clockwise. Sometimes you will see rotations in both directions in the same question, especially where similar shapes are used one inside the other.
- Rotations usually take place in multiples of 45°, so you can see rotations of 45°, 90°, 135°, 180°, 225°, 270° and 315°.

Rotation of a Single Shape
- The simplest rotation is that of a single shape.
- Look at these two triangles:

- You can tell that the second triangle is a rotation of the first. It is difficult to be sure how much it has been rotated as all the corner angles are the same.
- There will usually be more clues, possibly another shape around the triangle, or in one of the corners. There will also be more clues if you have got four images to work with rather than two.
- Now look at this pair of shapes. Since they are irregular, it is easier to see what happens when they are rotated:

- Use the centre of the box the shape is in. Pick two points on the shape and rotate them in your mind to see if you can match them to the second shape.
- Once you have matched the two points, use a third to check that you are right.
- In this case the shape has been rotated 45° clockwise.

Rotation of Shaded Segments

- In this sort of question, the overall shape might not appear to move because it is a regular shape.
- Look at this pair of shapes:

- The first step in identifying that the shaded segments have rotated is that you have the same number of each type of shading and you can find the same order going in the same direction.
- Match a segment in both shapes. In these two you can see there is just one shaded segment so they are easy to match.
- You should see that the rotation is 135° clockwise.
- Sometimes you will have more than one type of shading in a rotated shape.

Example
Look at this pair of images. What has happened from the first image to the second?

Match a segment in both shapes – try the white segment between the two grey ones as it is easy to track.
The segments have rotated 90° anti-clockwise.

Remember

A clockwise rotation of 270° is the same as an anti-clockwise rotation of 90°. This is a similar idea to looking at a clock face; 45 minutes past the hour is the same as 15 minutes to the hour.

Remember

You can always rotate the paper on your table if it helps.

Two Different Rotation Patterns

- In some questions, you may have two different rotations happening within one pair of images.

- Look at the rotations in the inner and outer segments of this shape:

- The outer segments have rotated 90° clockwise, but the inner segments have rotated 90° anti-clockwise.

- Occasionally, a second rotation is shown with a shape going around the shaded figure.

Quick Test

1. The first two images on the left are a pair. Work out which of the five images on the right completes the second pair in the same way as the first pair.

   a) is to as is to

       A   B   C   D   E

   b) is to as is to

       A   B   C   D   E

2. The first two boxes on the left are a pair. Work out which of the five boxes on the right completes the second pair in the same way as the first pair.

   a) is to as is to

       A   B   C   D   E

   b) is to as is to

       A   B   C   D   E

   c) is to as is to

       A   B   C   D   E

Spotting Patterns

You should be able to:

- spot the patterns in grid questions
- work out what the question is asking you to do
- apply changes from one shape to another.

What to Expect

- In this section we will look at questions in grid layouts. You will need to identify the patterns and continue them to find the answer.
- You can expect to have to spot at least two changes, so make sure you look at all of the images twice as it can be easy to miss something.
- The changes can be any connections, from size to shading, from number of shapes to number of sides.
- Reflections are one of the most common connections in grids as the layout can make them quite clear to see.
- In small grids, changes can go along the rows and down the columns.
- In large grids, changes can also go diagonally or use the whole grid.

Remember

As with all questions in the CEM test, working at speed is important for these types of question, but understanding what you are seeing is essential.

Skills in Spotting Patterns

Changes to Shapes

- A shape may simply change its size or its shading pattern. You could then be asked to apply that change to a different shape.
- Other changes you may see include:
  - position (for example, moving from one corner to another)
  - rotation (for example, twisting a quarter turn or half turn)
  - reflection.

Changes in Number of Items

- Another type of change could see the following:
  - An identical shape could be added.
  - A corner may be added to the shape.
  - The number of shapes in the box might double.

Combination of Shapes

- Lots of shapes could be put together as one item – let's call it a 'compound shape'. They may even end up looking like something that you recognise, such as a car or a boat.
- Here are some of the changes that may occur:
  - the shading of any of the component shapes (for example, the shading of the body or the headlights)

Change in Size

Change in Number

Combination of Shapes

- the shape of one of the components (for example, the headlights)
- the whole shape could be reflected (for example, if the car image on page 26 was reflected in a vertical line, the only thing that would appear to move is the steering wheel).

Interpreting the Changes

- Identifying the changes is only half of the question. You then have to apply those changes to a completely different shape.
- For example, if the main body of the car shown right changes to black shading, one of the answer options could present the boat with a black hull:

- If the car roof also changes to black shading, one of the answer options could present the boat with a black sail:

- If the car is also reflected, look for the sail of the boat being reflected in the answer options:

Working with Grids

- We will first look at some simple grids before building to the larger grids that you can expect in the test.

Example

Look at this simple grid. Three of the boxes have a shape in them and one is empty (marked '?'). What shape would you expect to complete the grid?

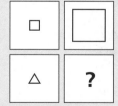

The 'key' box is the one that connects a completed row with a completed column. In this grid, it is the top left box with the small square.

Now you can look for similarities in both of the other filled boxes. Next to the small square is a big square. Underneath the small square is a small triangle. What is changing in the rows and columns?

- In the rows it is the size that changes.
- In the columns it is the shape that changes.

Now you can put the two rules together. What is the missing shape?

- The shape that fits the empty box must be a different size (row change) and a different shape (column change).
- It must be a bigger triangle.

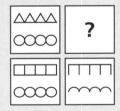

Remember

The trick to doing these questions is to spot which of the completed boxes are related to each other, what has changed and what has stayed the same.

- If each box in the grid contains several simple shapes, any of them could change in various ways.

Example

Look at this grid. How would you expect the empty box (marked '?') to be completed?

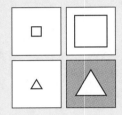

Remember

You might find it easier to work out what you think the empty box should contain by doing a sketch, especially when there is more than one change to think about. Then you can compare it with the possible answers you have been given.

In this grid, the 'key' box is the one at the bottom left corner. The box has four squares side by side above four circles. Now look at what is in the other boxes:

- There are the same four circles but with four triangles in the box above.
- There are four semi-circles and what looks like the squares but without the baselines in the box to the right.

What is changing in the rows and columns?

- There are changes to the shapes in both directions. In the columns the top shape has changed from squares to triangles.
- In the rows there are two things happening: the circles and the squares have both been altered.

Look carefully at the changes to the shapes in the rows. In the bottom right box, the circles have been cut in half to make semi-circles. The squares in the same box have lost their baselines. What should go in the empty box?

- To create the shape in the empty top right box you need to do the same.
- Cut the circles in half and remove the baselines from the triangles to create a zig-zag pattern.

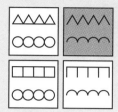

- Now let's consider a trickier example.

Example

Look at this grid. How would you expect the empty box (marked '?') to be completed?

The 'key' box in the bottom right has what looks like a sailing boat on the waves, with a sun in the sky. There are lots of shapes in there, but they look like something else, so you can use the 'picture' you can see to help you spot the changes.

This example contains reflections, shading changes and shape changes. You need to look at these changes one step at a time.

Look at the top right box to see how it can be turned into an image for the empty box:

- First you need to reflect the car – the steering wheel needs to move sides:

- Next the colour of the car body and roof needs to change:

- Finally, the sun will need to change into a moon and move to the other side of the box:

The missing box is a reflected black car at night.

Quick Test

In these questions, decide which of the boxes on the right can be used to complete the grid on the left.

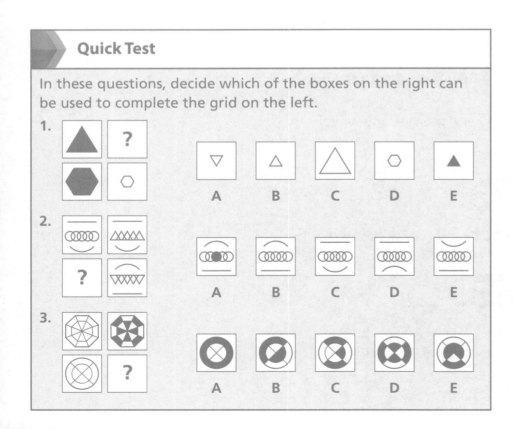

Simple 3 × 3 Grids

- In the CEM test, you are most likely to have to work with grids that are at least three columns by three rows in size (i.e. 3 × 3).
- There will be a combination of changes in 3 × 3 grids. Some changes will go across the rows and some changes will go down the columns or across the diagonals. You need to look for the different patterns these changes make.
- Here is a simple example:

Remember

There is often more than one rule to follow in these problems and you need to be able to exclude things that are put there to distract you.

> **Example**
> Look at this grid. How would you expect the empty box (marked '?') to be completed?
>
>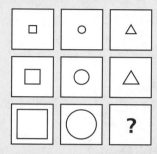
>
> One of the best places to start to look for patterns is with the **top box** of the **middle column**:
>
> - The shape in the top box of the middle column is a circle.
> - To the left is a square and to the right is a triangle.
> - None of the shapes are the same in this row, but they are the same size. You will need to look at other areas of the grid to see if there are any further similarities or patterns.
>
> If you cannot find a pattern across the rows of the grid, try looking down the columns:
>
> - Below the circle is a slightly bigger circle and below that circle is an even bigger circle.
> - The matching shapes and increasing sizes are two different possible patterns.
>
> Once you have spotted a pattern or patterns, you need to check the other columns in the grid to see if these patterns are repeated:
>
> - The first column is made up of a square that gets bigger and bigger.
> - The last column is made up of two triangles; the lower one is larger than the top one.
>
> The shape that fits the empty box must be a bigger triangle, to match the pattern of the other columns. It must also be the same size as the square and circle in that row.
>
>

Grids with a Reflection

- 3 × 3 grid questions may have a reflection pattern in them, but not necessarily from just one box to the next.
- The line of symmetry may go through the centre of the middle row or column.

Example

Look at this grid. How would you expect the empty box (marked '?') to be completed?

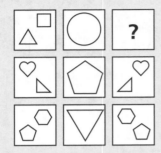

Although some of the boxes have more than one shape in them, the middle column has just one shape. This can be a clue that the pattern is symmetrical.

If you think the question is about symmetry, look for boxes that contain similar shapes:

- In this grid, both of the light grey boxes shown below have a heart and a right-angled triangle in them.
- Both of the darker grey boxes have a pentagon and a hexagon in them.

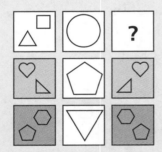

Once you have spotted the symmetrical pattern, it can be a good idea to mark the line of symmetry on the grid. It can be done quickly and doesn't need to be accurate as it is just there to help you think about the reflected shapes.

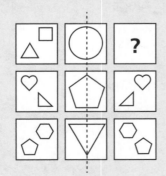

You should now be able to work out what should go into the empty box. In this grid it is a reflection of the top left box. It will be a square and a triangle – the square will be in the top left corner of the box and the triangle in the bottom right corner.

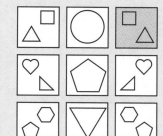

More Complex 3 × 3 Grids

- The patterns in some grids will be more difficult to spot. The changes can be more complicated or may go along diagonals rather than down columns or across rows.
- Working methodically will help you find the patterns so that you can complete the grid.

Skills for Grids with More than One Change

- As with the more simple 3 × 3 grids, start to look for patterns with the **top box** of the **middle column**.

Example

Look at this grid. How would you expect the empty box (marked '?') to be completed?

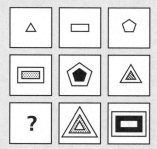

The shape in the top box of the middle column is a rectangle. To the left is a triangle, and to the right a pentagon. The shapes are all different in the top row, but they all have black outlines and no shading. You will need to look at other areas of the grid for further similarities and patterns.

If you cannot find a pattern across the rows of the grid, try looking down the columns. In the box below the rectangle are two pentagons, one inside the other. The inner one has black shading.

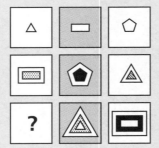

There are no obvious similarities here, so you will need to look in a different direction again. Patterns may appear diagonally on 3 × 3 grids so this is the next direction to look in.

In the box below and to the left of the rectangle there are two rectangles, one inside the other. The inner rectangle has a pattern but it is not the solid black shading as seen inside the pentagon – it is made up of small dots.

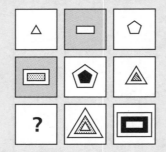

Even though the match doesn't seem to be exact, it is worth looking at other diagonals to see if there are any other clues to the pattern. There are three possible diagonal patterns going down and left in a 3 × 3 grid, and three more going down and right. It is worth looking at all of these when you are trying to find these patterns.

The box at the bottom right of the grid is also a rectangle (following the same diagonal pattern as the other rectangles), although this box has three rectangles, one inside another, and the middle one is shaded black.

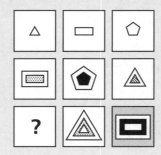

Each time you go down a row, the shape moves one column to the left and a similar shape is added around it. However, this doesn't explain the shading pattern.

Once you are satisfied that you have identified one pattern, move on to work out any others that you have spotted:

- The pentagons in the centre box and the rectangles in the bottom right box feature solid black shading.
- The rectangles in the middle row have a dotted pattern.
- The triangles in the bottom row also have a dotted pattern.

The patterns move across to the right as you progress down the rows. The triangles in the middle row have a diagonal striped pattern, which must be used in the missing shape.

So, putting everything together, the missing shape must be three pentagons – one inside another, and the second one should have a diagonal striped pattern.

Latin Squares

- A Latin square is a type of arrangement in which the same figures are repeated once in each column and once in each row.
- In a Latin square, the shape of the figures does not change.
- In the grid to the right, the quadrilateral appears once in each row/column. The spiral appears once in each row/column and the cross appears once in each row/column.

- Sometimes you might see a grid that combines Latin square elements with other features that change according to the rows or columns.
- In the grid to the right, there is a Latin square for the type of quadrilateral in each square: the square appears once in each row/column; the rectangle appears once in each row/column and the diamond appears once in each row/column.
- The shading changes depending on each column: the figures in the left-hand column are all white, the figures in the middle column are grey, and the figures in the right-hand column are all black.
- The dots in the bottom right-hand corner of each box change according to the column: the left-hand column has one dot; the middle column has two dots; the right-hand column has three dots.

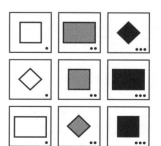

Different Shaped Grids

- Sometimes you may be presented with a different type of grid. You can still use the same skills to tackle those questions:

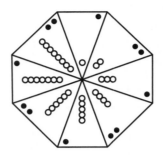

- Here, around the edge of the octagonal grid, there are alternately one and two black circles.
- In the middle of the grid, starting with the top central wedge, the number of white circles increases by one each time.

Quick Test

In these questions, decide which of the boxes on the right can be used to complete the grid on the left.

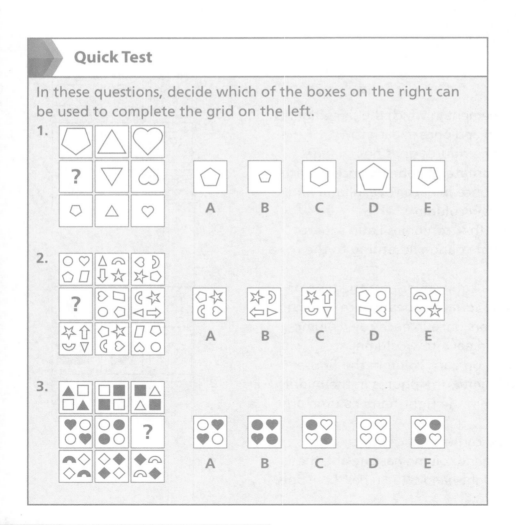

Completing Sequences

You should be able to:

- identify repeating patterns
- spot one-step and two-step patterns
- recognise changes based on number patterns.

What to Expect

- In these questions you might be shown five boxes: four with images in and one empty box labelled with a question mark. From the given options, you need to pick the correct box to complete the sequence.
- The trick to doing these questions is to find the change taking place from one box to the next.
- You could see these different types of sequences:
  - **Repeating patterns** (for example, shapes swapping back and forth from one box to the next)
  - **One-step patterns** (for example, the same change happens over and over again to build up a shape or to take one apart)
  - **Two-step patterns** (for example, two changes occur from one box to the next)
  - **Number patterns** (for example, the number of shapes changes from one box to the next).

Remember

These questions might take a little more time than some of the others. Try not to rush them, but don't be afraid to leave one and come back to it at the end.

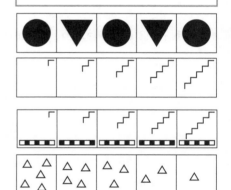

Repeating Patterns

- Repeating patterns make the same basic changes in every step.
- The pattern could be that one shape swaps to another and back again, or that the shading pattern swaps each time.
- In more complicated questions, shapes may be changed and rotated at each step.

Skills for Back and Forth Patterns

- When a pattern involves two shapes that swap, the change should be obvious.

> **Example**
> What is the repeating pattern shown here?
>
>
>
> The shape keeps swapping between a circle and a triangle, but nothing else is changing.

- Another repeating pattern may involve reflecting a shape in either a vertical or a horizontal mirror line and back again.

  Example

  What type of mirror line is being used in this repeating pattern?

  The triangle is being reflected in a horizontal mirror line.

- Sometimes a repeating pattern can be the shading of a shape swapping back and forth.

  Example

  What change is made each time to give this repeating pattern?

  The shape is always a circle but the shading swaps from black to white each time.

- It is possible that the shading **and** the shape will change.

  Example

  What is the repeating pattern in this sequence?

  The pattern swaps between a white circle and a shaded triangle each time.

> **Remember**
>
> Some of these questions might seem obvious, but take a few moments to look twice at each question just to be sure.

Skills for Building Up Patterns

- A repeated pattern could be used to add shapes to build a shape.

  Example

  What is the repeating pattern from left to right in this sequence?

  One circle is added in each box to the right of the previous circle.

- However, more elements may change at each step to build up a more complex repeating pattern.

  Example

  What is the repeating pattern from left to right in this sequence?

  There is one fewer circle in each box; each time the circle on the right is removed. At the same time, a white square is added in each box, and any existing squares turn black.

One-Step Patterns

- In these patterns you will see the same change happen in each box in the sequence. Once you have identified the change, you know what is happening.
- The change might affect:
  - the number of shapes
  - the size of shapes
  - the shading of shapes
  - the rotation of shapes
  - the shape of the figures.

Skills for Building a Shape

- In these types of question, you simply keep adding an identical block to build up a shape.

> **Example**
> Look at these five boxes. What should be in the empty box labelled with a question mark?
>
>
>
> The first box has two rows of black and white squares, the third box has four rows, the fourth box has five rows and the fifth box has six rows.
>
> A row is added each time at the bottom to continue the pattern; one row is white square before black square and the next is black square before white square, and so on.
>
> From this information you can work out that the second box should have three rows of black and white squares:
>
>

- Some questions are the other way round to construction questions. The sequence will look like you are removing the same piece each time.
- For example, here is the same question as above, but the boxes have been reversed:

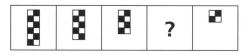

- The first box has six rows of black and white squares, the second box has five rows, the third box has four rows and the fifth box has just two rows.
- A row is removed each time from the bottom of the pattern. Logically, you can work out that the fourth box should have three rows of black and white squares.

Skills for Rotation

- A one-step pattern may involve a simple rotation.

Example

Look at these five boxes. What should be in the empty one?

In this example you can see a 90° clockwise rotation, so the missing shape is:

Skills for Moving a Shape

- In another kind of one-step pattern, a shape moves around inside the boxes.

Example

Look at these five boxes. What should be in the empty one?

Every box has a square and a circle in it.

The square does not move or change in any way (it is a distraction).

The circle moves from one corner to another in an anti-clockwise direction.

The empty box should have a circle in the top left corner, just like the fifth box:

> **Quick Test**
>
> Which of the images on the right can be used to complete the sequence in the boxes on the left?

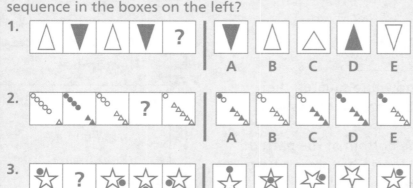

Two-Step Patterns

- Some questions may involve two or more changes.
- The changes might be a combination of any these:
  - number of shapes
  - size
  - shape
  - shading
  - rotation
  - reflection.

Skills for Building Shapes

- You may have to take into account two patterns at once.

> ### Example
> Look at these five boxes. What should be in the empty one?
>
>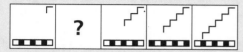
>
> The first box has two lines in the top right corner, joined together to make a right angle. It also has seven squares at the bottom that alternate between black and white.
>
> The third box has three sets of lines at right angles and the same seven squares at the bottom. Does that mean the empty box should have two sets of lines and the same squares?
>
> No, it doesn't. There are two boxes still to look at and the fourth one shows that the squares swap between black and white before swapping back for the fifth box.
>
> The correct answer is two sets of lines at right angles with seven black and white squares, starting with a black square:

Skills for Two Repeating Patterns

- Some questions may present two repeating patterns that overlap each other.
- Look at these five boxes and try to describe what is going on:

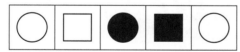

  - The shapes swap between a circle and a square.
  - The first circle and square are white; the second circle and square are black.
  - The last circle is also white.
  - There are two repeating patterns: one pattern changing the shape, and one pattern changing the shading.

Skills for Reversing Patterns

- Some patterns seem to reverse part way through.
- The simplest example of this sort of question is one where a single shape changes. Look at this complete pattern:

  - The circle changes into a triangle and then into a square.
  - After that, the pattern reverses and the square becomes a triangle and the triangle becomes a circle.

- Now look at this complete pattern and try to describe what is happening:

  - The shading seems to spread out from the middle into the outer segments in the first few boxes.
  - Once the shading is only in the outer segments, it reverses and heads back towards the middle again.
- This sort of question may have rotation as a second pattern, so keep an eye out for other connections and patterns. Unfortunately, that means there could be distractions as well.

Number Patterns

- Number patterns bring simple mathematical operations into questions involving sequences.
- The number of shapes in the sequence may change by:
  - adding the same number
  - subtracting the same number
  - multiplying by the same number.
- You may even see shapes changing according to common number patterns, such as square numbers (1, 4, 9, 16, 25, etc.) and triangular numbers (1, 3, 6, 10, 15, etc.).

Skills for Adding and Subtracting

- In these questions, the number of shapes changes by the same value each time.

Example

Look at these five boxes. What should be in the empty one?

You can see that the same shape is in each box a different number of times, so the first thing to do is count the shapes. The first box has one circle, the second has three, the third you have to work out, the fourth has seven and the last box has nine.

The difference between the first and second box is two, and the difference between the fourth and fifth boxes is two. Now that you have a possible rule, check to see if it works.

The second box has three circles, so adding two more will give you five. If you add two more to go to the fourth box you get seven, which is correct.

- Subtraction is the opposite of addition. In questions involving number patterns, subtraction is the same question as addition, just with the boxes in reverse order.

Remember

The total number of items is limited by the size of the boxes, so there shouldn't be more than 25 items in the box that has the most items.

Remember

Adding or subtracting two shapes each time will give you the sequence of odd or even numbers, depending on what you started with.

Remember

Rather than trying to remember how many are in each box, you can write a number above or below the box.

Example

Look at these five boxes. What should be in the empty one?

Once again, you have the same shape in each box.

The first box has six triangles, the second box has five, the third has four, the fourth box is the one you are trying to work out and the last box has two triangles.

Having three complete boxes in a row does make it a little easier as you can see the pattern more clearly. The number of triangles reduces by one in each box from left to right.

That means the empty box should have three triangles in it.

Skills for Multiplying

- If the number of items multiplies from one box to the next, you can expect it to be limited to the two or three times table due to the limited space in the boxes.

Example

Look at these five boxes. What should be in the empty one?

Once again, the same shape appears in each box.

The first box has one square in it, the second has two, the third has four and the fourth has eight. The fifth box is the one you need to work out.

The difference between the number of shapes in the first two boxes is one, between the second and third boxes it is two, and between the third and fourth boxes it is four.

The number of squares in each box is doubling each time, so there should be 16 squares in the last box.

Quick Test

Which of the images on the right is best used to complete the sequence in the boxes on the left?

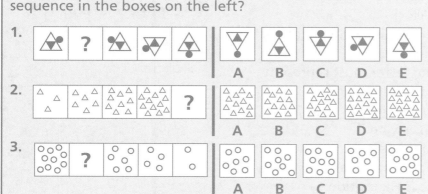

Breaking Codes

You should be able to:

- identify common letters and the features they represent
- work out the remaining code by matching up the remaining features.

Matching Letters to Characteristics

- In 'breaking codes' questions, you could be shown four images that each have a code of two or three letters.
- You will need to study the given images and work out what particular characteristic is represented by each letter.
- Once you have cracked the code, you need to choose the correct code for a fifth image.

> **Example**
> The four images on the left each have a code. Work out how the codes go with these images. Now find the correct code from the list on the right that matches the fifth image.
>
>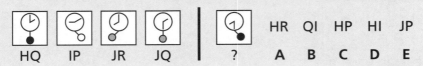
>
> | HQ | IP | JR | JQ | | ? | HR | QI | HP | HI | JP |
> |----|----|----|----|---|---|----|----|----|----|----|
> | | | | | | | **A** | **B** | **C** | **D** | **E** |

- First find a pair of common letters and identify the features:
  - The letter J is common to the third and fourth images.
  - JR is a clock with a grey pendulum that has swung to the left. The time is about eight o'clock.
  - JQ is a clock with a grey pendulum that is in the middle of its swing. The time is about half-past two.
- When you have identified the common feature, you can ignore the others and work out the rest of the code: H is a black pendulum; I is a white pendulum; J is a grey pendulum.
- You now know that the first letter is linked to the pendulum colour, so you can discount this feature for the second letter.
- The first and fourth images both have Q in their codes:
  - HQ is a clock with a black pendulum that is in the middle of its swing. The time is about two o'clock.
  - JQ is a clock with a grey pendulum that is in the middle of its swing. The time is about half-past two.
- All the images are clocks, so the second letter must represent the position of the pendulum, but not the shading of it:
  - P is a pendulum that has swung to the right.
  - Q is a pendulum in the middle of its swing.
  - R is a pendulum that has swung to the left.
- Now you have worked out the full code you can answer the question. The code for the fifth image is HP (option **C**).

> **Remember**
>
> Each letter can only code for a single characteristic (such as a black square), not multiple characteristics (for example, a black square beside a triangle in the top right-hand corner of a box).

> **Remember**
>
> Code questions often contain distractions to confuse you. Both the clock faces and the times in this example were distractions.

Codes with Three Letters

Example

The four images on the left each have a code. Work out how the codes go with these images. Now find the code from the list on the right that matches the fifth image.

RJW   SKW   RKY   TJX

   SJX   SKY   TKW   RSW   TJW

?   **A**   **B**   **C**   **D**   **E**

- Again, try to find two codes that only share the first letter.
- In the example, the codes for the first and third images both begin with the letter R. This tells you there is going to be something identical about them, so try to identify it:
  - RJW has white and grey outer segments with white and striped inner segments. The segments are in line with each other.
  - RKY has white and grey outer segments with white and black inner segments. The segments do not line up.
- It looks like R represents the white and grey outer segments. There are no other images with white and grey outer segments or other codes with an R, so this must be correct.
- As the first letter of the code must stand for a related feature, the remaining first letters mean: S for white and black outer segments; and T for white and striped outer segments.
- In this example, two images have K as the second letter of their code:
  - SKW has white and striped inner segments which are not in line with the outer segments.
  - RKY has white and black inner segments which are not in line with the outer segments.
- The common feature is that the segments are not in line with each other, so this is what K represents.
- Looking at the other images confirms that J stands for the segments being in line with each other.
- Follow the same process for the third letter. It will code for a different feature to the first two letters. In this example it stands for the shading of the inner segments: W is for white and striped; Y is for white and black; X is for white and grey.
- Now you can apply the full three-letter code to the fifth image.
- The image has white and striped segments on both the inside and outside, and the segments are in line with each other. The code for those features is TJW (option **E**).

Quick Test

1. Work out how the codes go with the four images on the left. Now find the correct code on the right for the fifth image.

   a)

   AM   CL   BM   CN

      AL   CM   BN   AN   BL

   ?   **A**   **B**   **C**   **D**   **E**

   b)

   EJX   DHY   DIZ   EJY

      DHZ   EHX   DJY   EIX   EHZ

   ?   **A**   **B**   **C**   **D**   **E**

Paper Folding and Identifying Shapes

You should be able to:

- imagine how a square piece of paper will look after being folded, holes punched in it and then unfolded
- find a given shape that is hidden within a more complex figure
- recognise how individual 2D shapes can be combined to create one larger shape.

Paper Folding and Hole Punching

- Paper folding and hole punching questions will show you a square piece of paper that has been folded several times.
- You will see that the paper has then had holes punched in it.
- You will need to work out what the unfolded paper would look like when it is opened out.

Example

Look at the square piece of paper on the left. It is folded and holes are punched in it. What would it look like when it is unfolded?

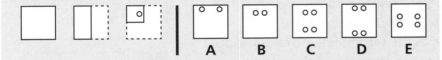

The paper has been folded in half vertically so both layers are on the left-hand side.

It has then been folded upwards into a quarter with all four layers of paper in the top left-hand corner of the original square.

Imagine the paper being unfolded, carrying out the reverse of what has been done. Try to imagine the holes appearing as the paper unfolds one step at a time:

- First the paper would unfold downwards so there would be two holes, aligned vertically:
- Then the paper would be unfolded again so the holes would be symmetrical in two vertically aligned columns:

Therefore the correct answer option is **C**.

Remember

The best way to become confident imagining how the paper will unfold is to practise folding and punching holes in some squares of paper yourself. Also look at how holes that are different shapes (for example hearts) change position as the paper unfolds.

Hidden Shapes

- Hidden shapes questions give a figure on the left-hand side and ask you to find that figure within one of the answer options shown on the right.
- The shape might be rotated in the correct answer option but it will not change in size or be reflected.

Example

Look at the given shape on the left. It is hidden in one of the images **A–E**. In which image is the shape hidden?

A **B** **C** **D** **E**

The figure given on the left-hand side of the question is hidden in answer option **A**:

> **Remember**
>
> Other lines can overlap with the given shape, but the shape itself must appear exactly as it is shown on the left-hand side of the question.

Make a Shape (2D)

- Make a shape (2D) tasks require you to look at a group of figures on the left-hand side of the question.
- You will need to imagine moving these figures to make one of the large shapes shown on the right-hand side of the question.
- The figures can be rotated and pushed together to form the larger shape.

Example

Which of the shapes on the right could be made from the figures on the left?

A **B** **C** **D** **E**

> **Remember**
>
> The figures on the left-hand side can be rotated to form the large shape on the right, but not reduced, enlarged or reflected.

The three figures could be rotated to make the shape in option **B**, so that is the correct answer:

Shapes on the right-hand side which would require extra figures in addition to those on the left cannot be correct. Here, the extra figure marked in grey would be needed to make option D, and the triangular piece would need reflecting, so that cannot be correct:

1. Look at the given shape on the left of each question. Choose the image (**A**, **B**, **C**, **D** or **E**) in which this shape is hidden.

   a)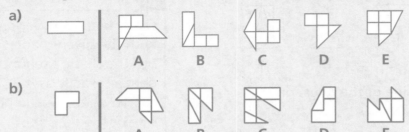

   b)

2. Look at each square of paper, which has been folded and holes punched through.

   Select the answer option (**A**, **B**, **C**, **D** or **E**) which shows how the square would appear when it is unfolded.

   a)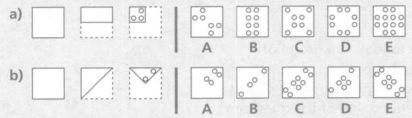

   b)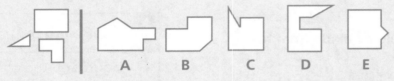

3. Which of the shapes on the right could be made from the figures on the left?

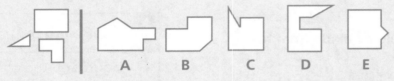

Nets of Cubes

You should be able to:

- imagine how a net folds to create a cube
- work out which faces will be opposite each other when a cube is formed
- spot how the figures on each face will align with one another.

What to Expect

- The net of a 3D shape is what it looks like if it is opened out flat.
- The net shows the faces and how they can fold up into the 3D shape.
- There are actually 11 different nets that will form a cube:

- In questions that require you to think about nets and cubes, you will see these different types of nets with patterns on the faces.
- You will need to think about how a cube would look when unfolded into a net, and also how a net would look when folded into a cube.
- Sometimes you will need to identify which faces are opposite one another when a net is folded.
- Some questions will require you to look very closely at exactly how the patterns on each face of the cube will touch when the net is folded.

Understanding Opposite Sides

- When you look at the net of a cube, one key skill you will need is the ability to quickly identify which faces are opposite one another when the net is folded up.
- The best way to practise this is by cutting some nets out of paper, folding them carefully and looking to see which faces are opposite one another when the cube is formed.
- It is also possible to spot which faces will be opposite each other just by looking at the net.
- In each of these nets, the two faces with the same figure on them would be opposite one another when the cube is formed:

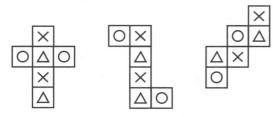

- In each cube, the crosses will be on opposite faces, the circles will be on opposite faces and the triangles will be on opposite faces.
- Note that in each of these nets, the faces with the same figure on them can **never touch** when the net is folded into a cube.

Understanding How a Net Folds Up

- You need to know how a net folds up to make a cube.

Example

Which cube can be made from the given net?

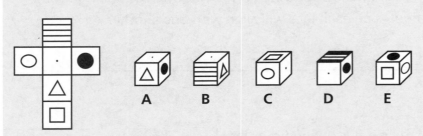

First look at the cubes to see if there are any figures that do not appear on the net. Here, option D has a bold black-striped face which isn't on the net, so you can quickly eliminate it.

Then look to eliminate cubes which show faces that would be opposite one another when the net is folded: the stripes and the triangle would be opposite one another; so would the dot and the square; and so would the oval and the black-shaded circle. Therefore you can eliminate options B, C and E.

The correct answer is option **A**.

- Pay close attention to which part of a face will come into contact with another face when the net is folded.
- Drawing on 3D cubes and turning them around helps to build up this skill, but you can also practise on 2D drawings.

Example

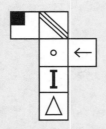

When folded, however the cube is rotated the arrow will point towards the circle and the three diagonal lines will meet where the arrow points to the circle.

Both of these views of the cube show how the net could be folded. Notice how the direction of the arrow and the stripes does not change in relation to each other.

Similarly, the pointed end of the triangle will always be next to the I shape; it does not matter how the cube is rotated.

Notice how the black square will not move to the opposite side of the cube from where it is shown. For example, this cube cannot be made:

Quick Test

1. a) Which of these are possible nets of a cube?

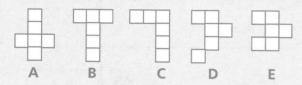

A   B   C   D   E

b) Why would the others not fold to make a cube?

2. Look at each net shown. Which cube could **not** be made from each net?

a)
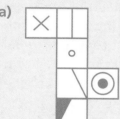

A   B   C   D   E

b)

A   B   C   D   E

3. Which net could be folded into each given cube?

a)

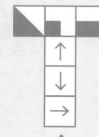    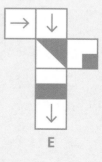

A   B   C   D   E

b)

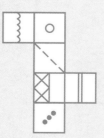 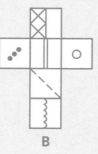 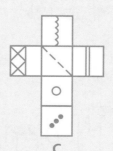 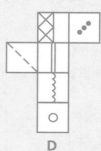 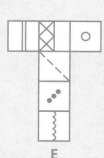

A   B   C   D   E

3D Figures

You should be able to:

- imagine how a 3D figure would look when it is viewed from one side
- recognise how 3D figures look when they are rotated
- imagine 3D figures being broken up into smaller blocks.

What to Expect

- Questions focused on 3D figures require you to look at them made from a series of blocks.
- The blocks can be cubes, cuboids, L-shaped, T-shaped or occasionally corner-shaped:

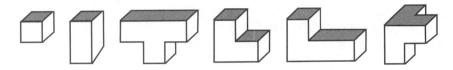

- The most common blocks are cubes and cuboids.
- The blocks will be stacked together to make a small model or figure. You will be able to see what shape of block has been used.
- It is a good idea to look at the orientation and arrangement of the blocks carefully to see how they have been positioned and how large each block is.
- You might be asked to select a top-down (plan) or side view of a 3D figure, so you will need to imagine looking at it from a different position:

PLAN VIEW

- Some questions could challenge you to imagine the 3D figure being rotated or turned:

- Other questions might ask you to imagine which set of blocks can be used to make a particular figure:

Understanding 2D Views of 3D Shapes

- You could be asked to select a 2D view of a 3D figure, either from one side or from above.
- You might be shown a figure made up of various blocks (usually cuboids and cubes) and be required to imagine what it would look like in 2D.

> **Example**
>
>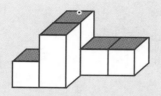
>
> Perhaps the easiest 2D view of the figure shown above is from the front. It would show one cube on the left-hand side, one cuboid to the right of it and two cubes arranged horizontally to the right of that:
>
> Notice how the 2D view does not distinguish between how far forward each block is. The 2D view does not show perspective.
>
> Now try to imagine the 2D view as if you were looking at the 3D figure from the right:
>
> The top-down (plan) view would show how the 3D figure looks when seen from above:
>
>
>
> Notice that the plan view, just like the other 2D views, shows the difference between the cube and the cuboid blocks but it does not distinguish how high they are.

Remember

Double check which side of the 3D figure you need to consider when finding the correct 2D view. Some questions might ask for a top-down (plan) view, whilst others could ask for a view from one side.

Remember

The top-down view always presumes you are approaching the figure from the front (i.e. through the page). You are not expected to imagine a top-down view when approaching the figure from behind or the side.

Understanding the Rotation of 3D Shapes

- You need to be able to imagine how a 3D figure would look if it were rotated.
- You will need to consider the individual shape of each block, as well as how the pieces have been combined to make the 3D shape.
- Each 3D figure can be rotated in several different ways, but the way the blocks are joined together cannot change.
- This figure has been rotated and shown from four different angles, but the way the blocks have been combined has not changed:

Remember

The figure can be rotated in any direction and therefore any side can be closest to you. Look out for all the possible rotations when you are considering answer options.

Example

Which of the options (A, B or C) shows this figure rotated?

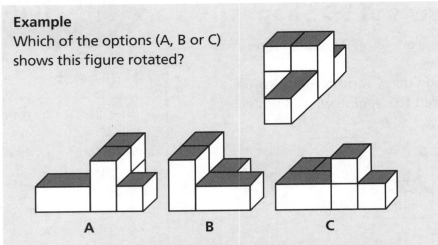

First look for any particularly prominent or noticeable blocks. Here, the taller blocks are in the middle of the 3D figure.

Using this taller section of the figure, you can eliminate option B straight away as the taller blocks are shown to one side of the figure.

Then consider how the remaining blocks are positioned.

In the given figure, the longer cuboid is at the front of the 3D shape. This cuboid appears on the left-hand side of option A, so you can be confident A is the correct answer.

Option C can be eliminated as the blocks are not arranged as they are in the original model (for example, the blocks on the back row are not in the correct positions).

Option **A** is the correct answer.

> **Remember**
>
> Use the prominent blocks to help you eliminate answer options that are clearly incorrect. Then look at the specific shape of each component part of the figure to decide between any remaining options.

Understanding 'Exploded' 3D Shapes

- You could be asked to imagine which component blocks could be used to create a 3D figure.
- Again, the shape of each individual block is important, so you will need to look closely at the shape of each part of the overall figure.
- You will need to identify which multiple-choice option shows the set of blocks that could be used to create the given 3D shape.
- This figure has been made by combining the following blocks:

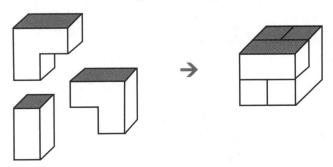

> **Remember**
>
> It is best to work methodically through these questions to eliminate incorrect answer options one at a time.

Example

Look at the figure shown on the right. Which set of blocks (A, B or C) could be used to make it?

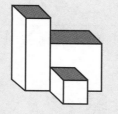

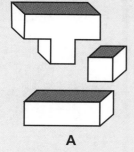
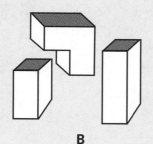
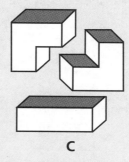

A   B   C

It is easiest to work by imagining rearranging each answer option in turn, rotating each block as if it were the piece of a 3D jigsaw.

In answer option A, the long cuboid could stand on end at the left-hand side of the given 3D figure. The cube could be placed next to it in the middle. However, the T-shaped block has no place in this figure, so you can eliminate option A.

In answer option B, the long cuboid could again stand on the end at the left. The short cuboid could be positioned with a square face facing forward, next to it. The L-shaped block could be positioned as balancing on the short cuboid.

Even though answer option B seems likely, you still need to check answer option C.

In option C, the long cuboid could again stand on the end at the left. One L-shaped block could stand on the right-hand side of the figure. In theory, the other L-shaped block could then tuck underneath it in the middle:

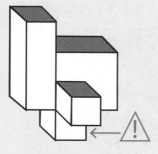

However, as the protruding lower section is not shown in the original figure, you can eliminate option C.

Therefore, the correct answer is **B**.

---

1. In these, find the top-down (plan) view of each 3D shape by choosing the correct option A, B, C, D or E.

   a)

                      A   B   C   D   E

   b)

   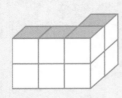 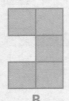 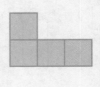 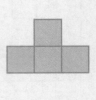

                      A   B   C   D   E

2. In these, decide which of the figures (A, B, C, D or E) would show what the given 3D figure would look like when rotated.

   a)

     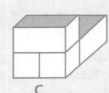  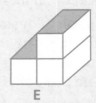

          A   B   C   D   E

   b)

   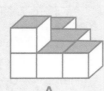 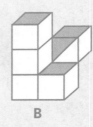 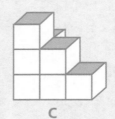  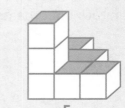

          A   B   C   D   E

3. Decide which set of blocks (A, B, C, D or E) could be used to create this 3D figure:

    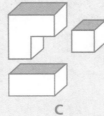  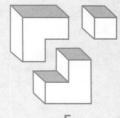

      A   B   C   D   E

Collins

11+
Non-Verbal Reasoning

Practice & Assessment

Workbook

Making Connections

Look at the five images in each row. Work out what connects **four** of the images and makes the other image the odd one out. Find the image **most unlike** the others.

Example i

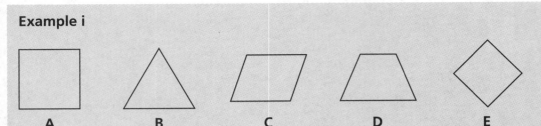

Shapes A, C, D and E all have four sides; shape B has three sides. The correct answer is **B**. This has already been marked in Example i for Practice Test 1 on your answer sheet on page 153.

Now have a go at these similar questions. Find the image **most unlike** the others.

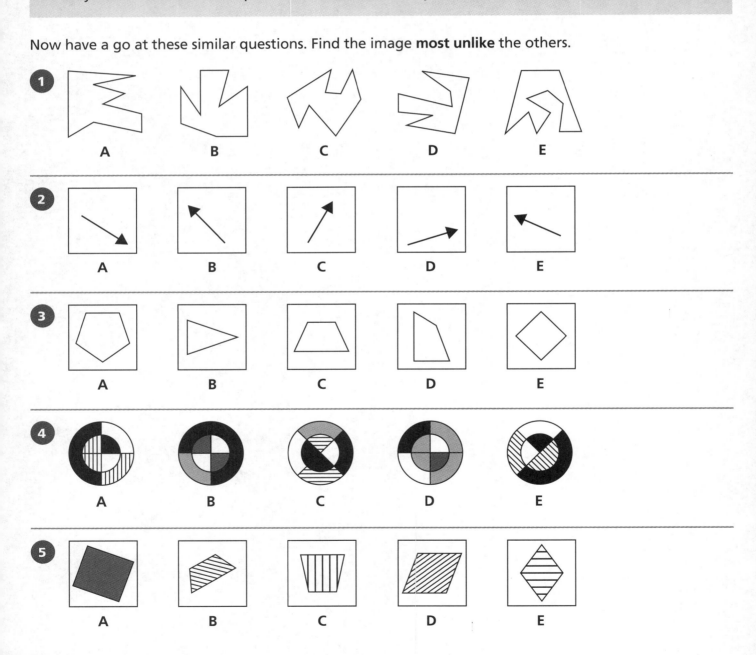

Look at the images on the left. Decide what makes these images similar to each other. Now find the image on the right (A, B, C, D or E) **most like** the images on the left.

Example ii

A B C D E

The two images on the left have identical arrowheads at both ends of the line. Only **B** has the same arrowhead at both ends so this is the correct answer. This has already been marked in Example ii for Practice Test 1 on your answer sheet on page 153.

Now have a go at these similar questions. Find the image **most like** those on the left.

 |

A B C D E

A B C D E

A B C D E

 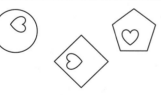

A B C D E

A B C D E

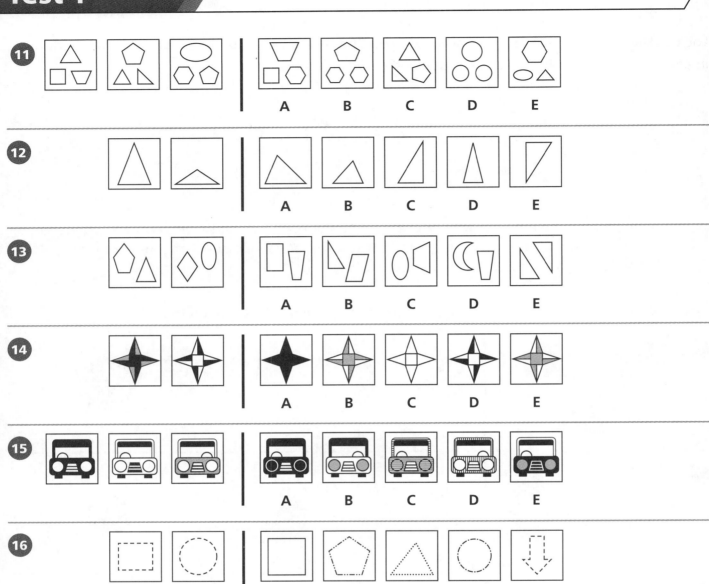

Finding Relationships

Look at the pair of images on the left. Work out how the two images go together. Now look at the third image. Work out which of the images (labelled A, B, C, D or E) on the right completes the second pair in the same way as the first pair.

Example

The second shape in each pair keeps the same shading and is reduced in size. The correct answer is **D**. This has already been marked in the Example for Practice Test 2 on your answer sheet on page 153.

Now have a go at these similar questions.

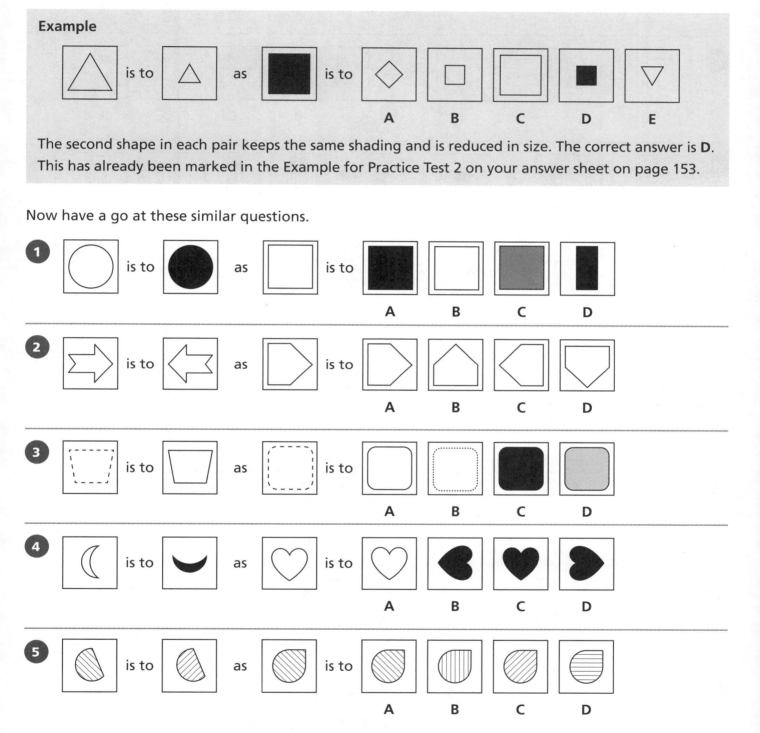

6 is to as is to

     A   **B**   **C**   **D**   **E**

7 is to as is to

     A   **B**   **C**   **D**   **E**

8 is to as is to

     A   **B**   **C**   **D**   **E**

9 is to as is to

     A   **B**   **C**   **D**   **E**

10 is to as is to

     A   **B**   **C**   **D**   **E**

11 is to as is to

     A   **B**   **C**   **D**   **E**

12 is to as is to

     A   **B**   **C**   **D**   **E**

13 is to as is to

     A   **B**   **C**   **D**   **E**

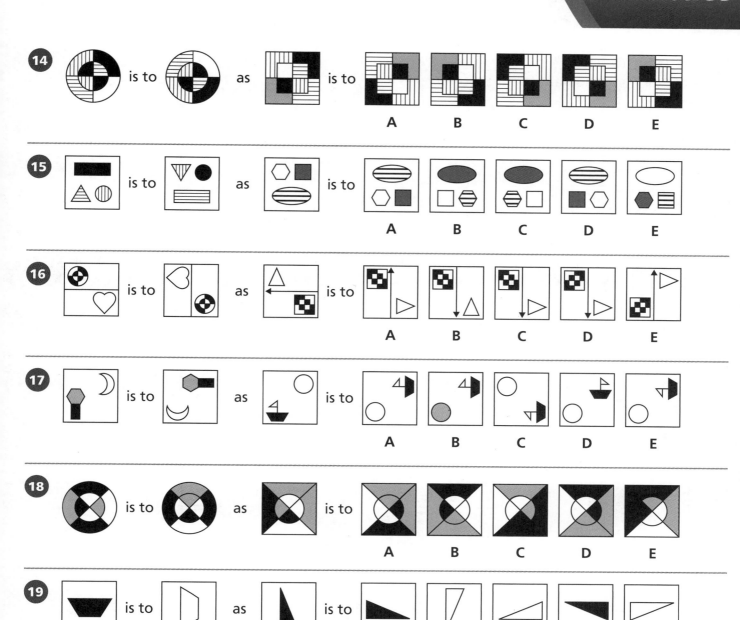

14 is to ... as ... is to ... A B C D E

15 is to ... as ... is to ... A B C D E

16 is to ... as ... is to ... A B C D E

17 is to ... as ... is to ... A B C D E

18 is to ... as ... is to ... A B C D E

19 is to ... as ... is to ... A B C D E

END OF TEST

Look at the set of pictures on the left. The picture marked with '?' is missing. Pick one of the pictures (A, B, C, D or E) on the right that **best** completes the set.

Example

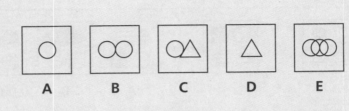

A   B   C   D   E

As the shapes in the boxes move from right to left, they double in number. The correct answer is **B**. This has already been marked in the Example for Practice Test 3 on your answer sheet on page 153.

Now have a go at these similar questions.

1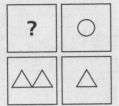

A   B   C   D   E

2

A   B   C   D   E

3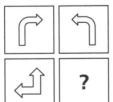

A   B   C   D   E

4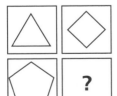

A   B   C   D   E

5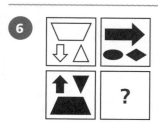

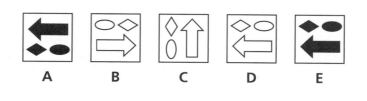

A   B   C   D   E

6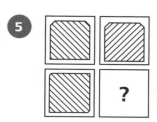

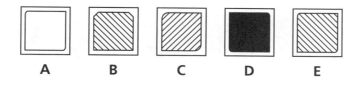

A   B   C   D   E

7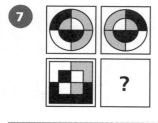

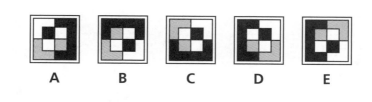

A   B   C   D   E

8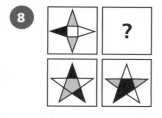

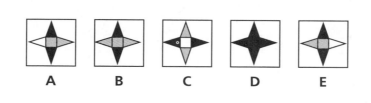

A   B   C   D   E

9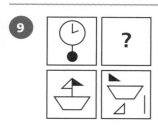

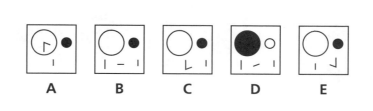

A   B   C   D   E

10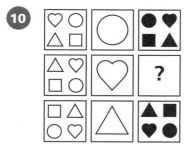

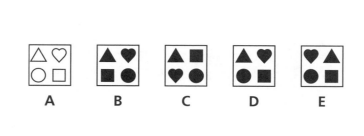

A   B   C   D   E

11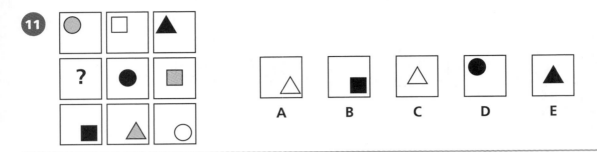

12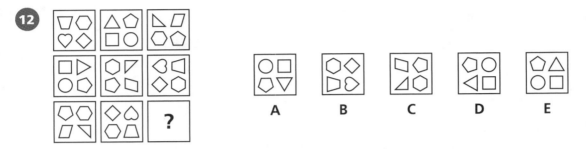

13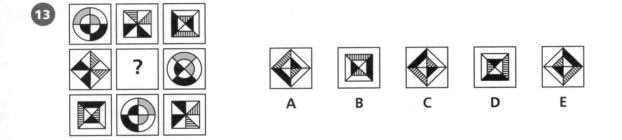

14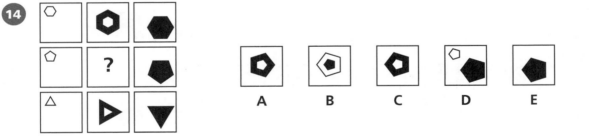

END OF TEST

One of the five boxes on the right completes the sequence or pattern on the left. Find the correct option, A, B, C, D or E.

Example

   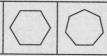

A   **B**   **C**   **D**   **E**

Looking at the boxes from left to right, the number of sides on the shape increases by one each time. The correct answer is **C**. This has already been marked in the Example for Practice Test 4 on your answer sheet on page 153.

Now have a go at these similar questions.

1

A   **B**   **C**   **D**   **E**

2

A   **B**   **C**   **D**   **E**

3

A   **B**   **C**   **D**   **E**

4

A   **B**   **C**   **D**   **E**

5

A   **B**   **C**   **D**   **E**

6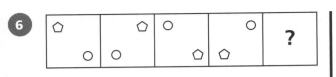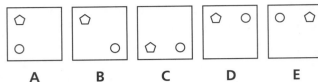

7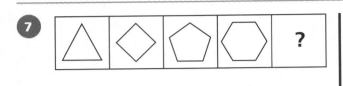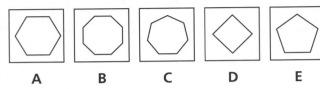

8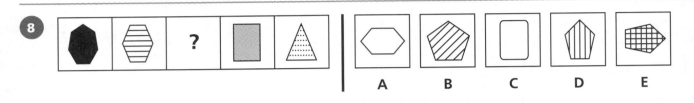

9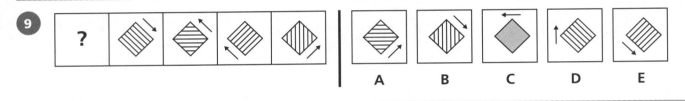

10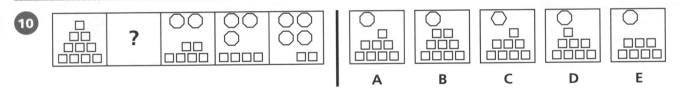

11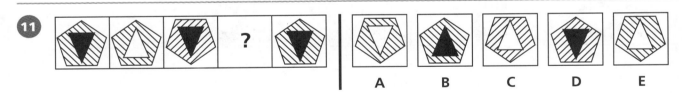

12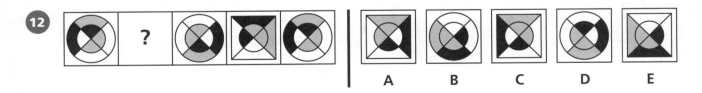

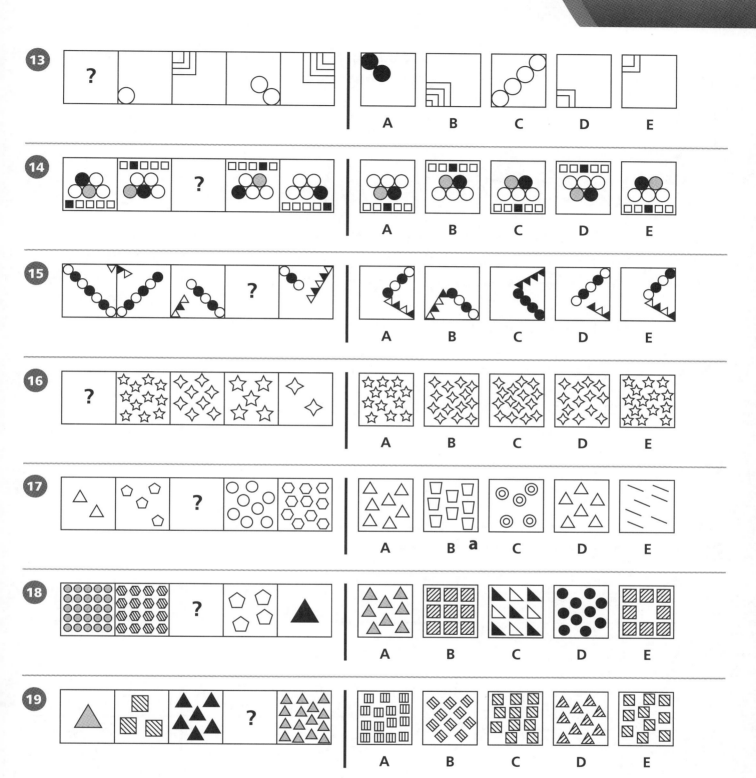

END OF TEST

The four images on the left each have a code. Work out how the codes go with these images. Now find the correct code from the list on the right that matches the fifth image.

Example

KS   LT   MT   LR   MS

?   A   B   C   D   E

The fifth shape is a circle and has a striped pattern. A circle has the letter code L. A striped pattern has the letter code T. The answer is **B**. This has already been marked in the Example for Practice Test 5 on your answer sheet on page 154.

Now have a go at these similar questions. Find the code that matches the fifth image.

1

CO   BP   AP   BO   CN

?   A   B   C   D   E

2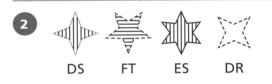

FR   ET   ER   FS   DT

?   A   B   C   D   E

3

QS   RU   PU   QT   RP

?   A   B   C   D   E

4

GJ   EK   FJ   GL   FL

?   A   B   C   D   E

5

DP   EO   FP   DO   FQ

?   A   B   C   D   E

6

UA   WB   VC   WC   UB

?   A   B   C   D   E

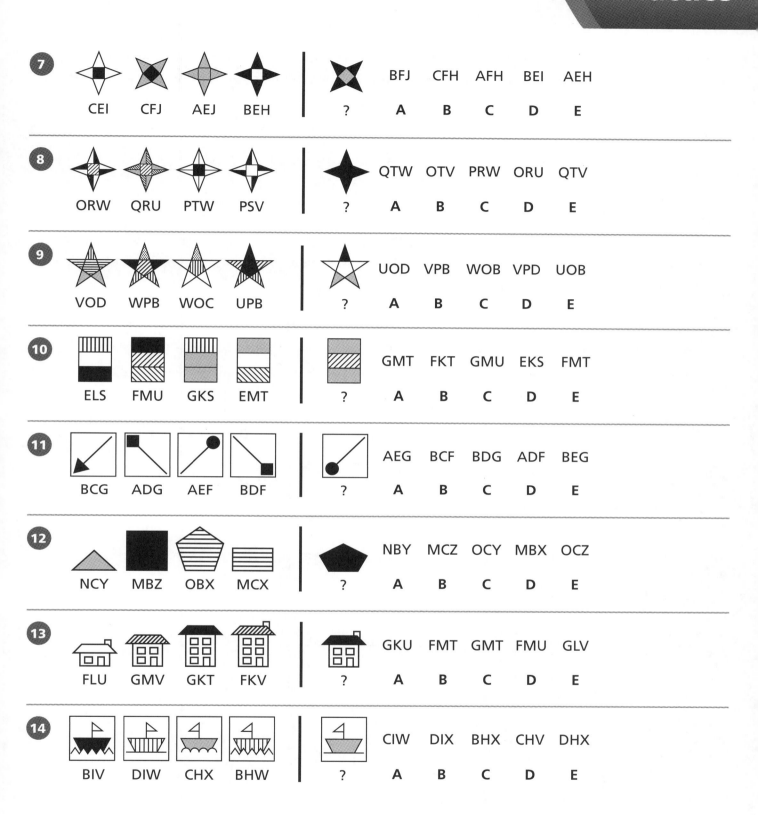

7

CEI   CFJ   AEJ   BEH

	BFJ	CFH	AFH	BEI	AEH
?	A	B	C	D	E

8

ORW   QRU   PTW   PSV

	QTW	OTV	PRW	ORU	QTV
?	A	B	C	D	E

9

VOD   WPB   WOC   UPB

	UOD	VPB	WOB	VPD	UOB
?	A	B	C	D	E

10

ELS   FMU   GKS   EMT

	GMT	FKT	GMU	EKS	FMT
?	A	B	C	D	E

11

BCG   ADG   AEF   BDF

	AEG	BCF	BDG	ADF	BEG
?	A	B	C	D	E

12

NCY   MBZ   OBX   MCX

	NBY	MCZ	OCY	MBX	OCZ
?	A	B	C	D	E

13

FLU   GMV   GKT   FKV

	GKU	FMT	GMT	FMU	GLV
?	A	B	C	D	E

14

BIV   DIW   CHX   BHW

	CIW	DIX	BHX	CHV	DHX
?	A	B	C	D	E

END OF TEST

Look at the square of paper shown on the left. Look at how it has been folded and some holes punched through. Imagine the paper has been unfolded. Select the answer option that shows what it would look like.

Example i

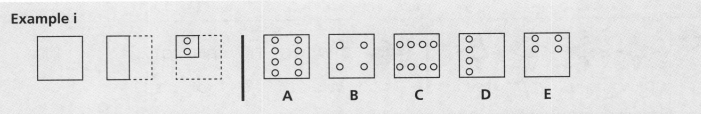

The square has been folded into quarters and the holes punched. When unfolded, it would look like option **A**, so this is the correct answer. This has already been marked in Example i for Practice Test 6 on your answer sheet on page 154.

Now have a go at these similar questions. Each square on the left has been folded and holes punched through. Select the option that shows how it would look when unfolded.

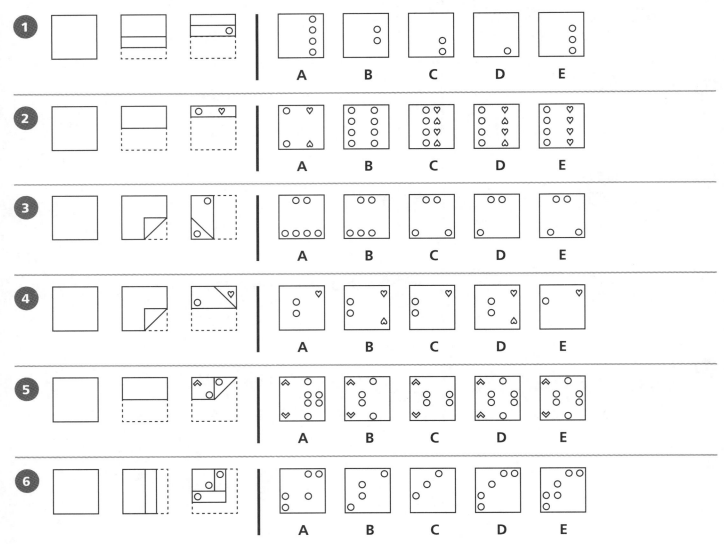

Look at the shape in each question. It is hidden in one of the answer options A, B, C, D or E. Select the answer option in which the given shape is hidden.

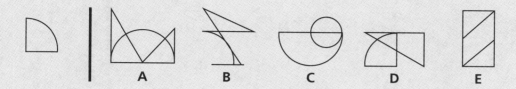

Example ii

The hidden shape is a quarter circle. It appears only in option D, so **D** is the correct answer. This has already been marked in Example ii for Practice Test 6 on your answer sheet on page 154.

Now have a go at these similar questions. Select the answer option in which the given shape is hidden.

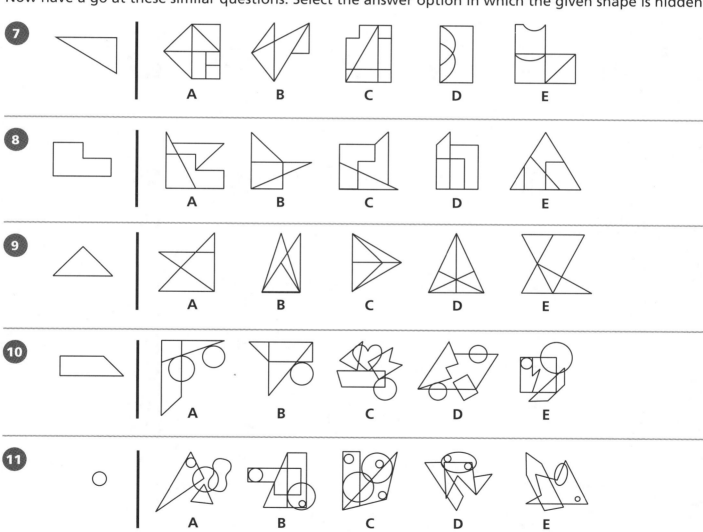

END OF TEST

Look at the given net. Select the answer option that shows the cube that can be made from the given net.

Example i

A   **B**   **C**   **D**   **E**

The double-headed arrow will point to the cross and the white circle. The triangle will point to the double-headed arrow. Therefore the answer is **C**. This has already been marked in Example i for Practice Test 7 on your answer sheet on page 154.

Now have a go at these similar questions.

1

   A   **B**   **C**   **D**   **E**

2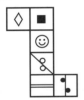

   A   **B**   **C**   **D**   **E**

3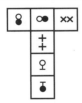

   A   **B**   **C**   **D**   **E**

4

   A   **B**   **C**   **D**   **E**

5

   A   **B**   **C**   **D**   **E**

In these questions, look at the net of the cube. One face has been selected. Decide which face would be opposite the given face when the net is folded.

Example ii

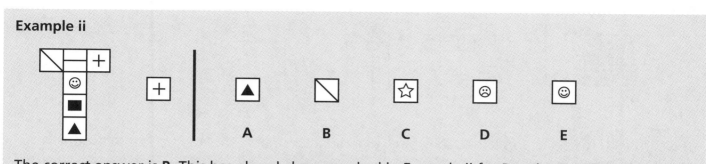

The correct answer is **B**. This has already been marked in Example ii for Practice Test 7 on your answer sheet on page 154.

Now have a go at these similar questions.

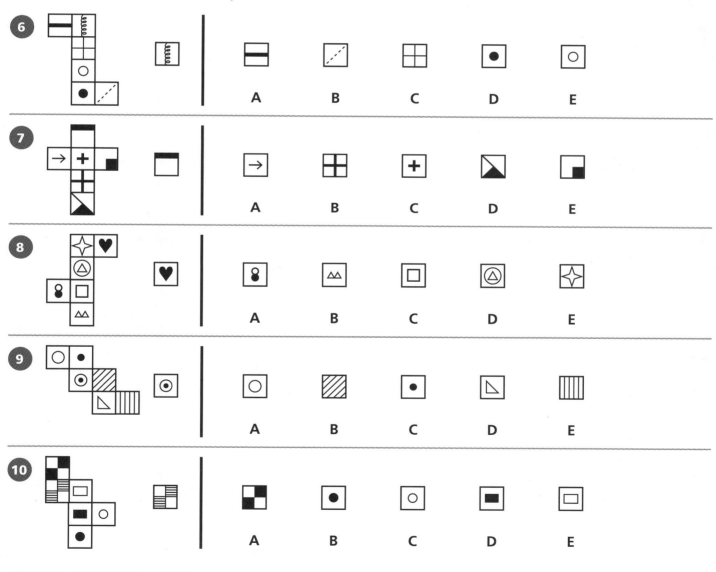

END OF TEST

Select how the following 3D figure would appear in a top-down (plan) view.

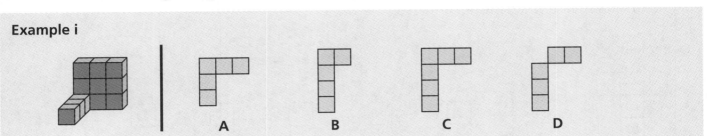

Example i

The correct answer is **C**. This has already been marked in Example i for Practice Test 8 on your answer sheet on page 154.

Now have a go at these similar questions. Select how each 3D figure would appear in a top-down (plan) view.

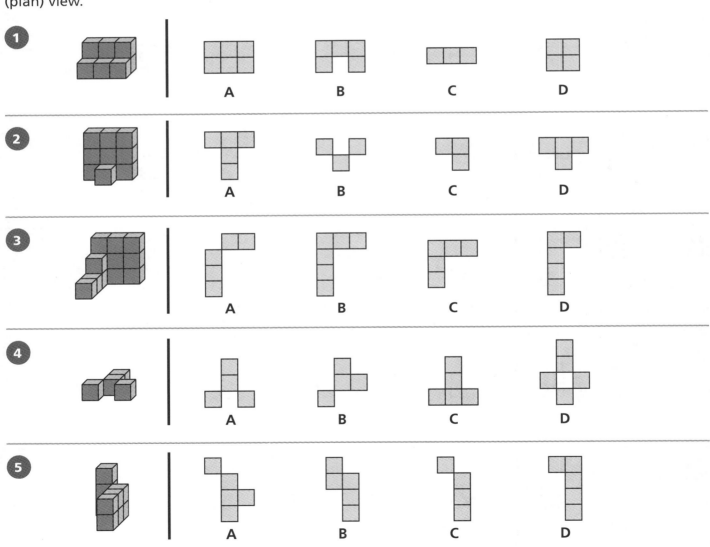

Decide which group of blocks (A, B, C, D or E) could be used to make the figure shown on the left.

Example ii

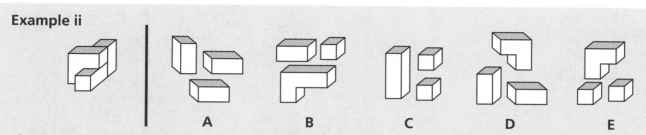

The correct answer is **D**. This has already been marked in Example ii for Practice Test 8 on your answer sheet on page 154.

Now have a go at these similar questions. Decide which group of blocks could be used to make the figure on the left.

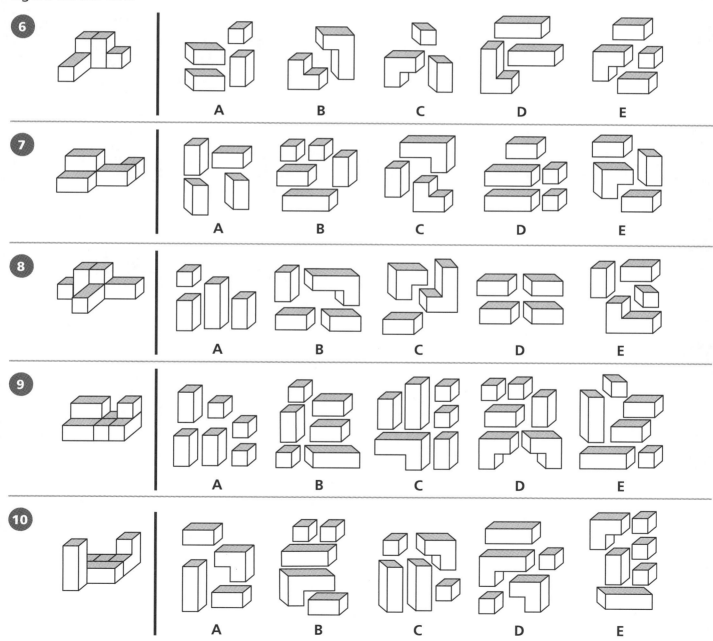

Which of the figures (A, B or C) would show the shape on the left when it is rotated?

Example iii

 |

A   B   C

The correct answer is **B**. This has already been marked in Example iii for Practice Test 8 on your answer sheet on page 154.

Now have a go at these similar questions.

 11 |

A   B   C

 12 |

A   B   C

13 |

A   B   C

14 |

A   B   C

15 |

A   B   C

END OF TEST

Collins

Non-Verbal Reasoning Assessment Paper 1

Instructions:

1. Ensure you have pencils and an eraser with you.

2. Make sure you are able to see a clock or watch.

3. Write your name on the answer sheet.

4. Do not open the question booklet until you are told to do so by an adult.

5. Mark your answers on the answer sheet only.

6. All workings must be completed on a separate piece of paper.

7. You should not use a calculator, dictionary or thesaurus at any point in this paper.

8. Move through the sections as quickly as possible and with care.

9. Follow the instructions at the foot of each page.

10. You should mark your answers with a horizontal strike, as shown on the answer sheet.

11. If you want to change your answer, ensure that you rub out your first answer and that your second answer is clearly more visible.

12. You can go back and review any questions that are within the section you are working on only.

You should await further instructions before moving onto another section.

Symbols and Phrases used in the Tests

 Instructions
 Time allowed for this section
 Stop and wait for further instructions
 Continue working

SECTION 1: VIEWS OF 3D FIGURES

 INSTRUCTIONS

🕐 **YOU HAVE 8 MINUTES TO COMPLETE THE FOLLOWING SECTION.**

YOU HAVE 15 QUESTIONS TO COMPLETE WITHIN THE TIME GIVEN.

Example i

Select how the following 3D figure would appear in a top-down (plan) view.

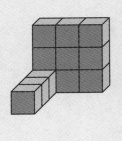 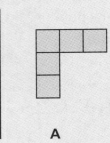 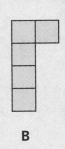 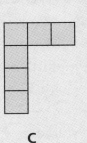 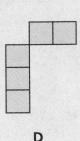 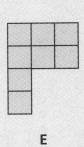

     A   **B**   **C**   **D**   **E**

The correct answer is **C**. This has already been marked in Example i in Section 1 of your answer sheet on page 155.

Example ii

Select how the following 3D figure would appear in a top-down (plan) view.

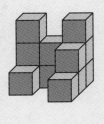 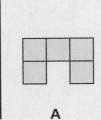 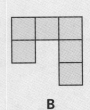 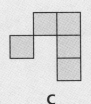 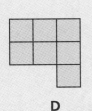 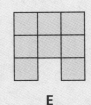

     A   **B**   **C**   **D**   **E**

The correct answer is **B**. Mark the answer B in Example ii in Section 1 of your answer sheet on page 155.

STOP AND WAIT FOR FURTHER INSTRUCTIONS

In each question, select how the 3D figure shown on the left would appear in a top-down (plan) view.

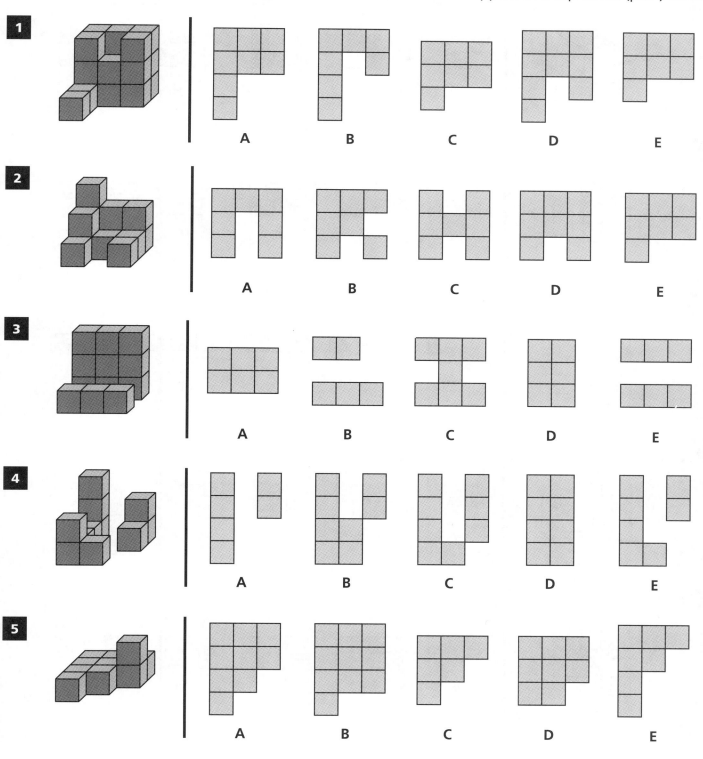

6

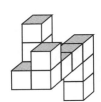 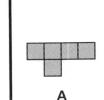 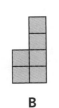 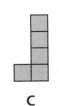

A B C D E

7

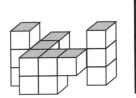 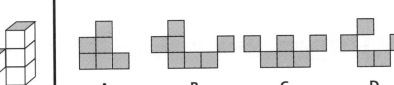 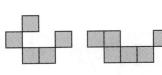

A B C D E

8

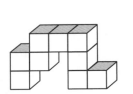   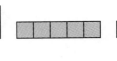

A B C D E

9

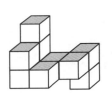

A B C D E

10

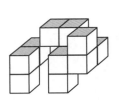

A B C D E

CONTINUE WORKING ➡

11

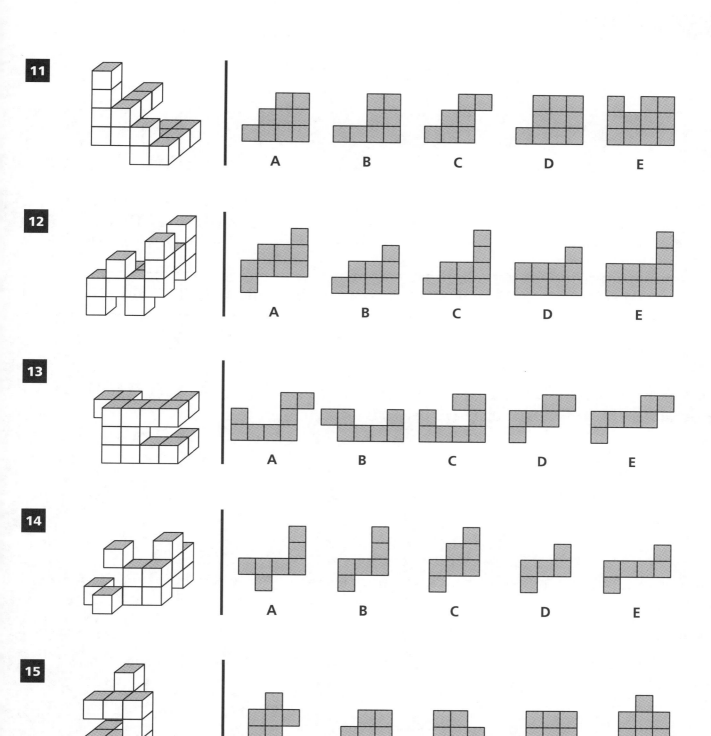

A   B   C   D   E

12

A   B   C   D   E

13

A   B   C   D   E

14

A   B   C   D   E

15

A   B   C   D   E

STOP AND WAIT FOR FURTHER INSTRUCTIONS

SECTION 2: COMPLETE THE GRID

 INSTRUCTIONS

 YOU HAVE 8 MINUTES TO COMPLETE THE FOLLOWING SECTION.

YOU HAVE 15 QUESTIONS TO COMPLETE WITHIN THE TIME GIVEN.

Example i

Look at the set of pictures on the left. The picture marked with '?' is missing. Pick one of the pictures from A–E on the right that **best** completes the set.

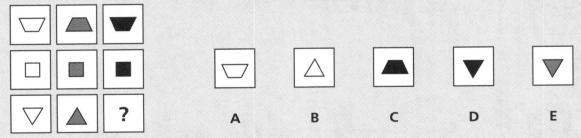

The correct answer is **D**. This has already been marked in Example i in Section 2 of your answer sheet on page 155.

Example ii

Look at the set of pictures on the left. The picture marked with '?' is missing. Pick one of the pictures from A–E on the right that **best** completes the set.

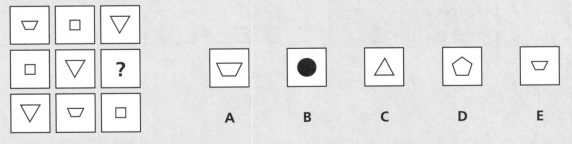

The correct answer is **E**. Mark the answer E in Example ii in Section 2 of your answer sheet on page 155.

STOP AND WAIT FOR FURTHER INSTRUCTIONS

In each question, look at the set of pictures on the left. The picture marked with '?' is missing. Pick one of the pictures from A–E on the right that **best** completes the set.

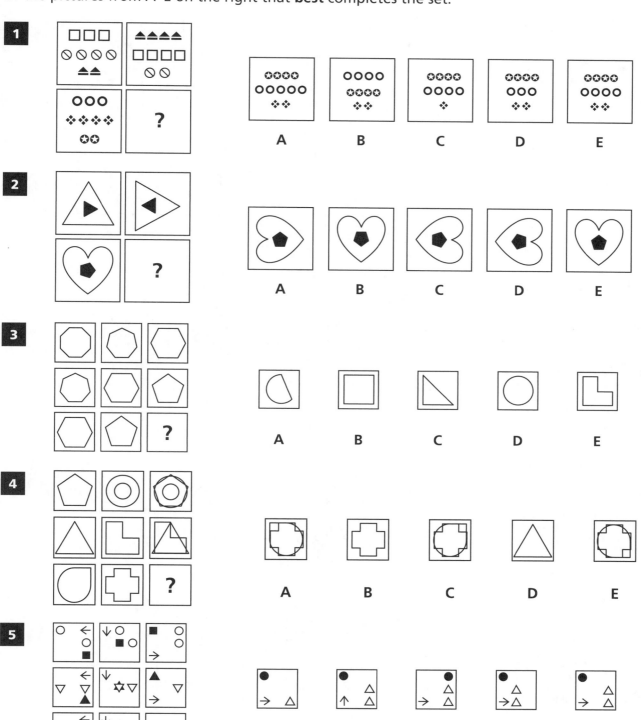

6
 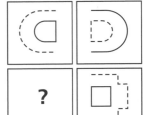
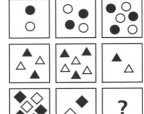

A   B   C   D   E

7

A   B   C   D   E

8

A   B   C   D   E

9

A   B   C   D   E

10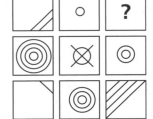

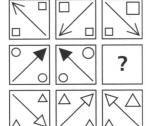

A   B   C   D   E

CONTINUE WORKING ⟹

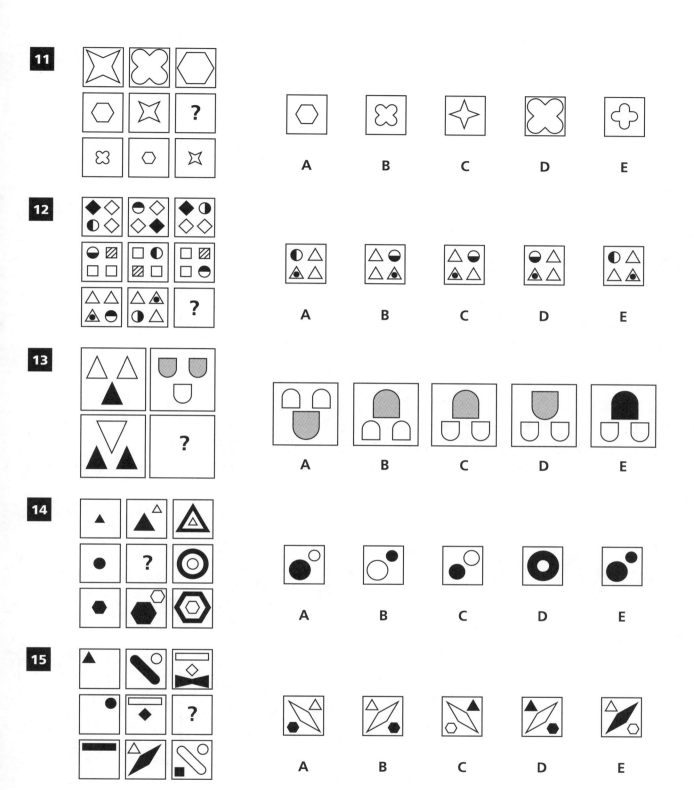

END OF PAPER

THIS PAGE HAS DELIBERATELY BEEN LEFT BLANK

Collins

Non-Verbal Reasoning
Assessment Paper 2

Instructions:

1. Ensure you have pencils and an eraser with you.

2. Make sure you are able to see a clock or watch.

3. Write your name on the answer sheet.

4. Do not open the question booklet until you are told to do so by an adult.

5. Mark your answers on the answer sheet only.

6. All workings must be completed on a separate piece of paper.

7. You should not use a calculator, dictionary or thesaurus at any point in this paper.

8. Move through the sections as quickly as possible and with care.

9. Follow the instructions at the foot of each page.

10. You should mark your answers with a horizontal strike, as shown on the answer sheet.

11. If you want to change your answer, ensure that you rub out your first answer and that your second answer is clearly more visible.

12. You can go back and review any questions that are within the section you are working on only.

You should await further instructions before moving onto another section.

Symbols and Phrases used in the Tests

 Instructions   Time allowed for this section   Stop and wait for further instructions   Continue working

SECTION 1: COMPLETE THE SEQUENCE

 ⚠ INSTRUCTIONS ⚠

🕐 **YOU HAVE 8 MINUTES TO COMPLETE THE FOLLOWING SECTION.**

YOU HAVE 15 QUESTIONS TO COMPLETE WITHIN THE TIME GIVEN.

Example i

Select the correct picture from the row on the right to replace the box marked '?' and finish the incomplete sequence on the left.

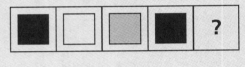

A   B   C   D   E

The correct answer is **A**. This has already been marked in Example i in Section 1 of your answer sheet on page 156.

Example ii

Select the correct picture from the row on the right to replace the box marked '?' and finish the incomplete sequence on the left.

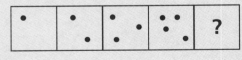

A   B   C   D   E

The correct answer is **D**. Mark the answer D in Example ii in Section 1 of your answer sheet on page 156.

STOP AND WAIT FOR FURTHER INSTRUCTIONS

Select the correct picture from the row on the right to replace the box marked '?' and finish the incomplete sequence on the left.

1

2

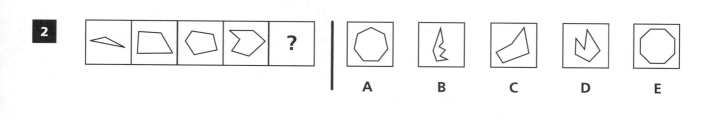

3

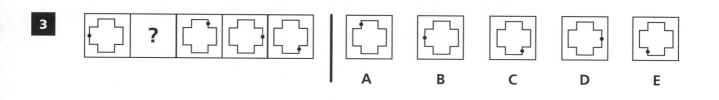

4

5

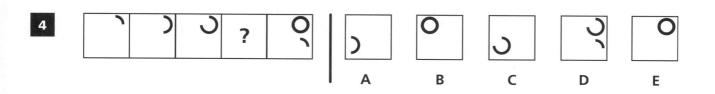

CONTINUE WORKING

6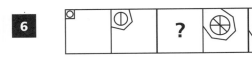

A   B   C   D   E

7

A   B   C   D   E

8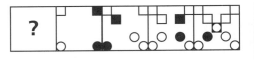

A   B   C   D   E

9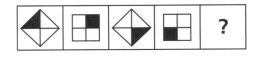

A   B   C   D   E

10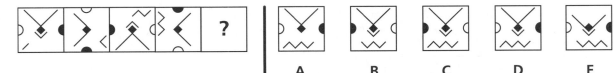

A   B   C   D   E

CONTINUE WORKING

11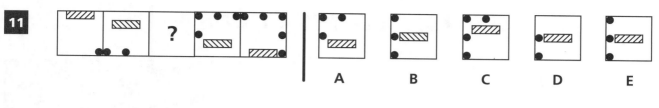

12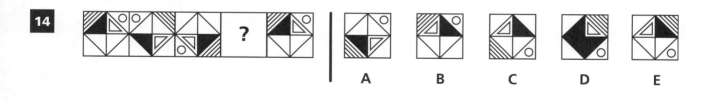

13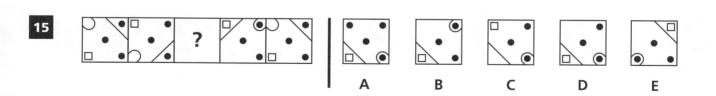

14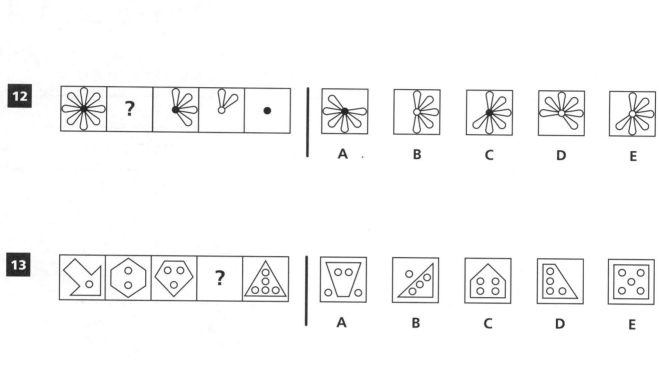

15

STOP AND WAIT FOR FURTHER INSTRUCTIONS

SECTION 2: CONNECTIONS

 YOU HAVE 8 MINUTES TO COMPLETE THE FOLLOWING SECTION.

YOU HAVE 15 QUESTIONS TO COMPLETE WITHIN THE TIME GIVEN.

Example i

Look at the two shapes on the left immediately below. Find the connection between them and apply it to the third shape.

 is to as is to

                         A   B   C   D   E

The correct answer is **C**. This has already been marked in Example i in Section 2 of your answer sheet on page 156.

Example ii

Look at the two shapes on the left immediately below. Find the connection between them and apply it to the third shape.

 is to as is to

                         A   B   C   D   E

The correct answer is **D**. Mark the answer D in Example ii in Section 2 of your answer sheet on page 156.

STOP AND WAIT FOR FURTHER INSTRUCTIONS

In these questions, look at the two shapes on the left. Find the connection between them and apply it to the third shape.

 is to as is to

A   **B**   **C**   **D**   **E**

2

 is to as is to

A   **B**   **C**   **D**   **E**

3

 is to as is to

A   **B**   **C**   **D**   **E**

4

 is to as is to

A   **B**   **C**   **D**   **E**

5

 is to as is to

A   **B**   **C**   **D**   **E**

CONTINUE WORKING ⇨

6 is to as is to

A　B　C　D　E

7 is to as is to

A　B　C　D　E

8 is to as is to

A　B　C　D　E

9 is to as is to

A　B　C　D　E

10 is to as is to

A　B　C　D　E

CONTINUE WORKING

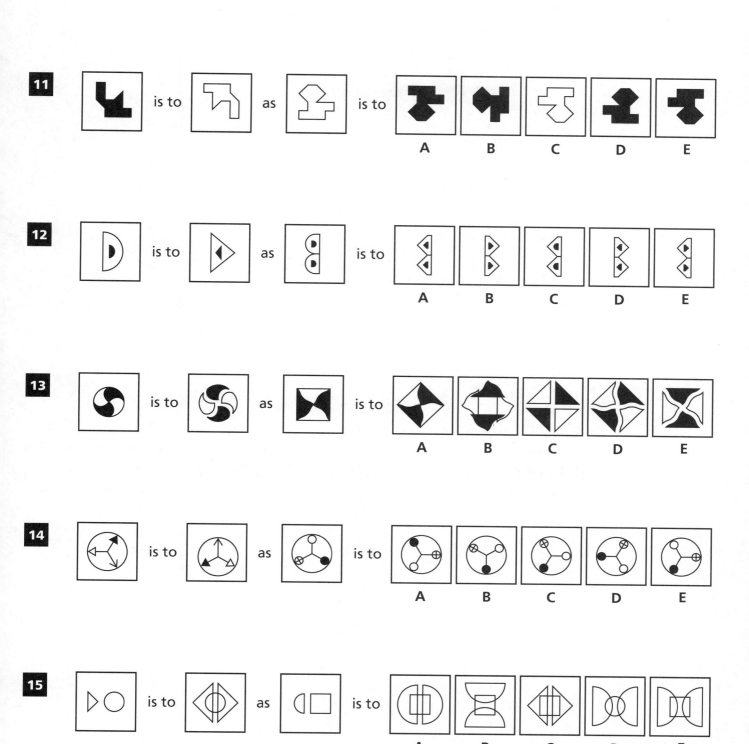

THIS PAGE HAS DELIBERATELY BEEN LEFT BLANK

Collins

Non-Verbal Reasoning
Assessment Paper 3

Instructions:

1. Ensure you have pencils and an eraser with you.

2. Make sure you are able to see a clock or watch.

3. Write your name on the answer sheet.

4. Do not open the question booklet until you are told to do so by an adult.

5. Mark your answers on the answer sheet only.

6. All workings must be completed on a separate piece of paper.

7. You should not use a calculator, dictionary or thesaurus at any point in this paper.

8. Move through the sections as quickly as possible and with care.

9. Follow the instructions at the foot of each page.

10. You should mark your answers with a horizontal strike, as shown on the answer sheet.

11. If you want to change your answer, ensure that you rub out your first answer and that your second answer is clearly more visible.

12. You can go back and review any questions that are within the section you are working on only.

You should await further instructions before moving onto another section.

Symbols and Phrases used in the Tests

 Instructions   Time allowed for this section   Stop and wait for further instructions   Continue working

SECTION 1: LEAST SIMILAR

 INSTRUCTIONS

 YOU HAVE 8 MINUTES TO COMPLETE THE FOLLOWING SECTION.

YOU HAVE 15 QUESTIONS TO COMPLETE WITHIN THE TIME GIVEN.

Example i

Select the figure that is least similar to the other figures.

A   B   C   D   E

The correct answer is **B**. This has already been marked in Example i in Section 1 of your answer sheet on page 157.

Example ii

Select the figure that is least similar to the other figures.

A   B   C   D   E

The correct answer is **A**. Mark the answer A in Example ii in Section 1 of your answer sheet on page 157.

STOP AND WAIT FOR FURTHER INSTRUCTIONS

In each question, select the figure that is least similar to the other figures.

A B C D E

A B C D E

A B C D E

A B C D E

A B C D E

CONTINUE WORKING

6

    A   B   C   D   E

7

    A   B   C   D   E

8

    A   B   C   D   E

9

    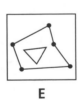

    A   B   C   D   E

10

    A   B   C   D   E

CONTINUE WORKING ⇨

11

A   B   C   D   E

12

A   B   C   D   E

13

A   B   C   D   E

14

A   B   C   D   E

15

A   B   C   D   E

STOP AND WAIT FOR FURTHER INSTRUCTIONS

SECTION 2: NETS OF CUBES

 INSTRUCTIONS

 YOU HAVE 8 MINUTES TO COMPLETE THE FOLLOWING SECTION.

YOU HAVE 15 QUESTIONS TO COMPLETE WITHIN THE TIME GIVEN.

Example i

Look at the cube net below. Select the only cube that could be formed from the net.

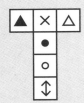

A   B   C   D   E

The correct answer is **C**. This has already been marked in Example i in Section 2 of your answer sheet on page 157.

Example ii

Look at the cube net below. Select the only cube that could be formed from the net.

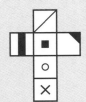

A   B   C   D   E

The correct answer is **E**. Mark the answer E in Example ii in Section 2 of your answer sheet on page 157.

STOP AND WAIT FOR FURTHER INSTRUCTIONS

In these questions, look at the net on the left. Select the only cube (A, B, C, D or E) that could be formed from the net.

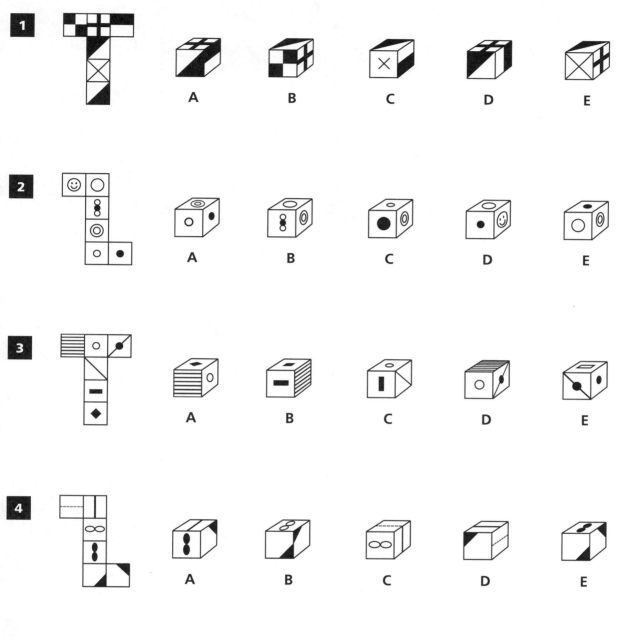

6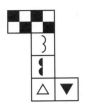

  A   **B**   **C**   **D**   **E**

7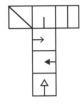

  A   **B**   **C**   **D**   **E**

8

  A   **B**   **C**   **D**   **E**

9

  A   **B**   **C**   **D**   **E**

10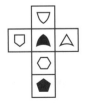

  A   **B**   **C**   **D**   **E**

CONTINUE WORKING

11

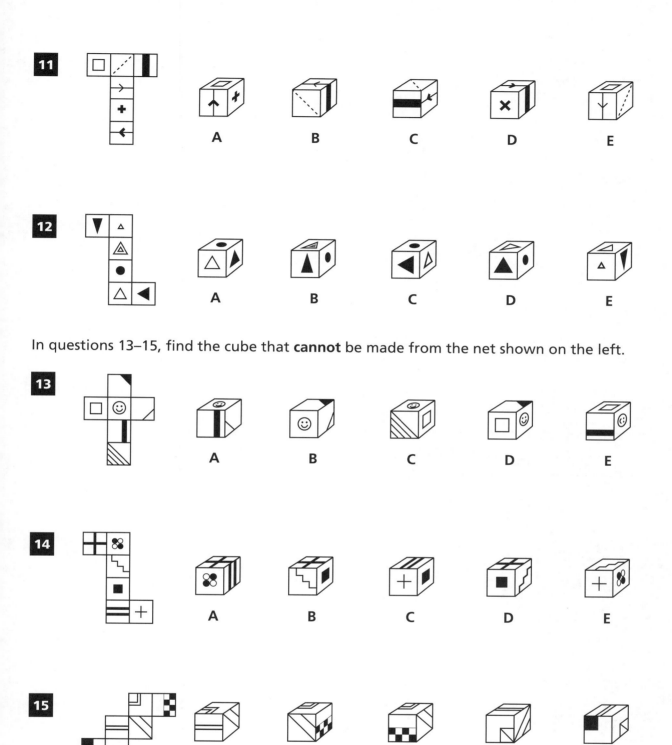

12

In questions 13–15, find the cube that **cannot** be made from the net shown on the left.

13

14

15

END OF PAPER

THIS PAGE HAS DELIBERATELY BEEN LEFT BLANK

Collins

Non-Verbal Reasoning Assessment Paper 4

Instructions:

1. Ensure you have pencils and an eraser with you.

2. Make sure you are able to see a clock or watch.

3. Write your name on the answer sheet.

4. Do not open the question booklet until you are told to do so by an adult.

5. Mark your answers on the answer sheet only.

6. All workings must be completed on a separate piece of paper.

7. You should not use a calculator, dictionary or thesaurus at any point in this paper.

8. Move through the sections as quickly as possible and with care.

9. Follow the instructions at the foot of each page.

10. You should mark your answers with a horizontal strike, as shown on the answer sheet.

11. If you want to change your answer, ensure that you rub out your first answer and that your second answer is clearly more visible.

12. You can go back and review any questions that are within the section you are working on only.

You should await further instructions before moving onto another section.

Symbols and Phrases used in the Tests

 Instructions

 Time allowed for this section

 Stop and wait for further instructions

 Continue working

SECTION 1: ROTATION

 INSTRUCTIONS

 YOU HAVE 8 MINUTES TO COMPLETE THE FOLLOWING SECTION.

YOU HAVE 15 QUESTIONS TO COMPLETE WITHIN THE TIME GIVEN.

Example i

Select one of the images below that is a rotation of the image on the left.

A   B   C   D   E

The correct answer is **C**. This has already been marked in Example i in Section 1 of your answer sheet on page 158.

Example ii

Select one of the images below that is a rotation of the image on the left.

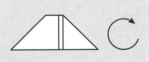 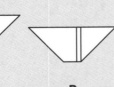

A   B   C   D   E

The correct answer is **E**. Mark the answer E in Example ii in Section 1 of your answer sheet on page 158.

STOP AND WAIT FOR FURTHER INSTRUCTIONS

In these questions, select one of the images (A, B, C, D or E) that is a rotation of the image on the left.

1

2

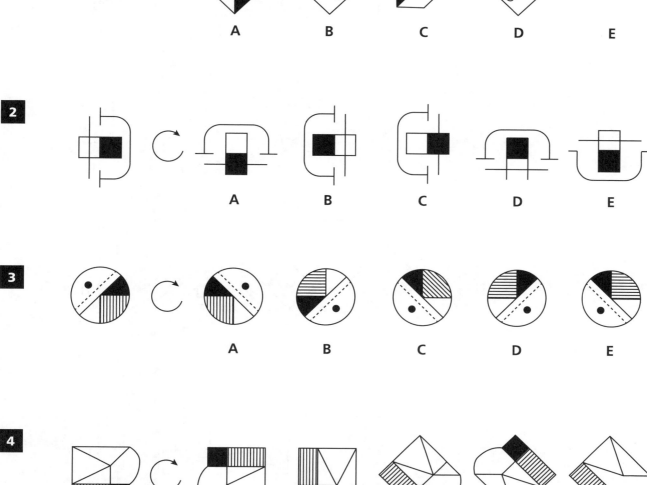

3

4

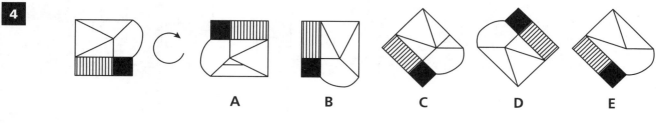

5

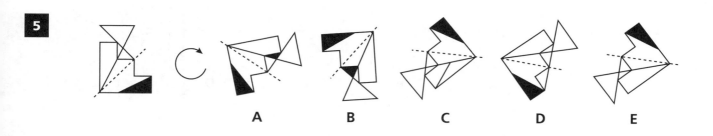

CONTINUE WORKING

6

A   B   C   D   E

7

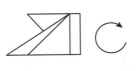

A   B   C   D   E

8

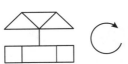 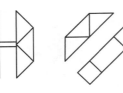

A   B   C   D   E

9

   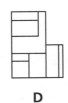

A   B   C   D   E

10

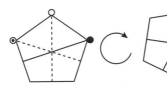 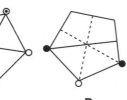

A   B   C   D   E

CONTINUE WORKING

A   B   C   D   E

A   B   C   D   E

A   B   C   D   E

A   B   C   D   E

A   B   C   D   E

STOP AND WAIT FOR FURTHER INSTRUCTIONS

SECTION 2: REFLECTION

YOU HAVE 8 MINUTES TO COMPLETE THE FOLLOWING SECTION.

YOU HAVE 15 QUESTIONS TO COMPLETE WITHIN THE TIME GIVEN.

Example i

Select how the shape or pattern on the left would appear when reflected in the dashed line.

A   B   C   D   E

The correct answer is **E**. This has already been marked in Example i in Section 2 of your answer sheet on page 158.

Example ii

Select how the shape or pattern on the left would appear when reflected in the dashed line.

A   B   C   D   E

The correct answer is **C**. Mark the answer C in Example ii in Section 2 of your answer sheet on page 158.

STOP AND WAIT FOR FURTHER INSTRUCTIONS

In these questions, select how the given shape or pattern would appear when reflected in the dashed line.

1

 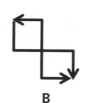 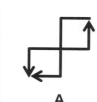

A   B   C   D   E

2

A   B   C   D   E

3

A   B   C   D   E

4

A   B   C   D   E

5

   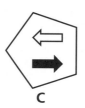  

A   B   C   D   E

CONTINUE WORKING

6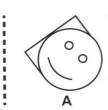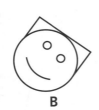

A   B   C   D   E

7

A   B   C   D   E

8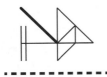

A   B   C   D   E

9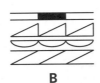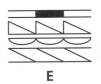

A   B   C   D   E

10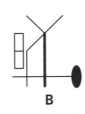

A   B   C   D   E

CONTINUE WORKING ➡

11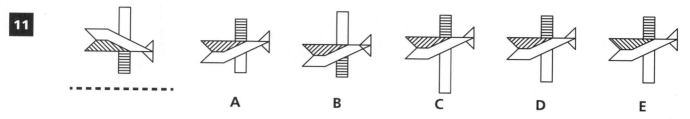

In these questions, select an image (A, B, C, D or E) that shows how the given shape or pattern will appear when reflected.

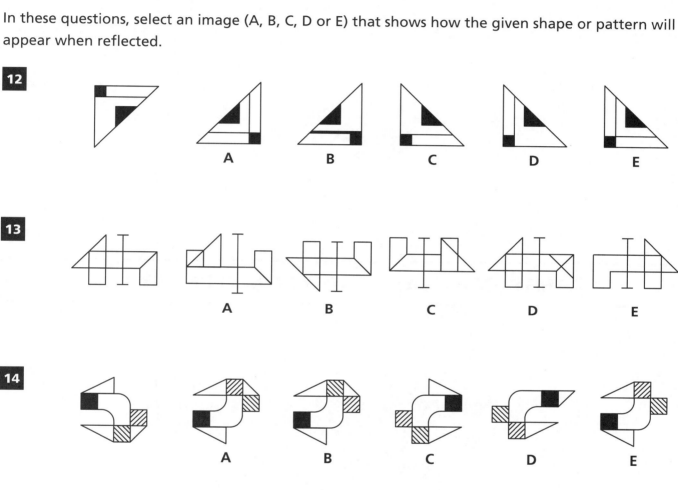

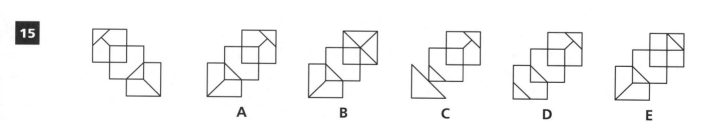

THIS PAGE HAS DELIBERATELY BEEN LEFT BLANK

Collins

Non-Verbal Reasoning Assessment Paper 5

Instructions:

1. Ensure you have pencils and an eraser with you.

2. Make sure you are able to see a clock or watch.

3. Write your name on the answer sheet.

4. Do not open the question booklet until you are told to do so by an adult.

5. Mark your answers on the answer sheet only.

6. All workings must be completed on a separate piece of paper.

7. You should not use a calculator, dictionary or thesaurus at any point in this paper.

8. Move through the sections as quickly as possible and with care.

9. Follow the instructions at the foot of each page.

10. You should mark your answers with a horizontal strike, as shown on the answer sheet.

11. If you want to change your answer, ensure that you rub out your first answer and that your second answer is clearly more visible.

12. You can go back and review any questions that are within the section you are working on only.

You should await further instructions before moving onto another section.

Symbols and Phrases used in the Tests

 Instructions   Time allowed for this section   Stop and wait for further instructions   Continue working

SECTION 1: MOST SIMILAR

 INSTRUCTIONS

 YOU HAVE 8 MINUTES TO COMPLETE THE FOLLOWING SECTION.

YOU HAVE 15 QUESTIONS TO COMPLETE WITHIN THE TIME GIVEN.

Example i

The three figures on the left are similar in some way. Work out how they are similar and select the figure from the right that goes with them.

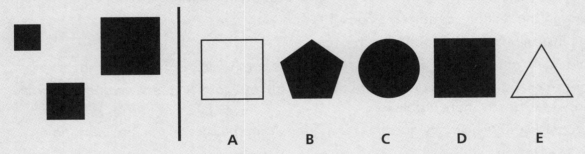

The correct answer is **D**. This has already been marked in Example i in Section 1 of your answer sheet on page 159.

Example ii

The three figures on the left are similar in some way. Work out how they are similar and select the figure from the right that goes with them.

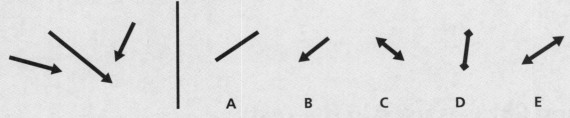

The correct answer is **B**. Mark the answer B in Example ii in Section 1 of your answer sheet on page 159.

STOP AND WAIT FOR FURTHER INSTRUCTIONS

In these questions, the three figures on the left are similar in some way. Work out how they are similar and select the figure (A, B, C, D or E) that goes with them.

1

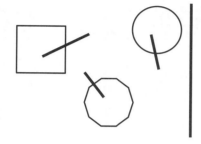

$$\frac{4}{8} \qquad \frac{8}{10} \qquad \frac{2}{9} \qquad \frac{5}{3} \qquad \frac{7}{10}$$

A   B   C   D   E

2

A   B   C   D   E

3

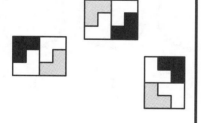

A   B   C   D   E

4

A   B   C   D   E

5

A   B   C   D   E

CONTINUE WORKING

6

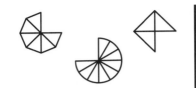

A   B   C   D   E

7

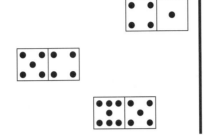

A   B   C   D   E

8

A   B   C   D   E

9

A   B   C   D   E

10

←↖↑↗

↗→↘↓

↘↓↙←

←↖↙↓   ↙←↖↑↗   ↘→↗↑   ←→↑↓   ↑↗→↘

A   B   C   D   E

CONTINUE WORKING ⟹

In these questions, which of the patterns (A, B, C, D or E) belongs in the group within the oval?

11

A   B   C   D   E

12

A   B   C   D   E

13

A   B   C   D   E

14

A   B   C   D   E

15

A   B   C   D   E

STOP AND WAIT FOR FURTHER INSTRUCTIONS

SECTION 2: ROTATED 3D FIGURES

 ⚠ INSTRUCTIONS ⚠

🕐 **YOU HAVE 8 MINUTES TO COMPLETE THE FOLLOWING SECTION.**

YOU HAVE 15 QUESTIONS TO COMPLETE WITHIN THE TIME GIVEN.

Examples i and ii

Look at figures A and B shown on the left below. They are then rotated. Match the two rotations shown on the right to each of the original figures A and B.

Example i   **Example ii**

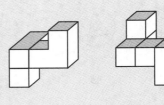

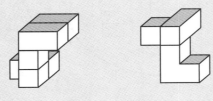

A   **B**

Example i

The correct answer is **B**. This has already been marked in Example i in Section 2 of your answer sheet on page 159.

Example ii

The correct answer is **A**. Mark the answer A in Example ii in Section 2 of your answer sheet on page 159.

STOP AND WAIT FOR FURTHER INSTRUCTIONS

Match the rotations shown in questions 1–5 to one of the original figures A, B, C, D or E.

A B C D E

1   A   B   C   D   E

2   A   B   C   D   E

3   A   B   C   D   E

4   A   B   C   D   E

5   A   B   C   D   E

CONTINUE WORKING ⇨

Match the rotations shown in questions 6–10 to one of the original figures A, B, C, D or E.

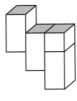

A   B   C   D   E

6   A   B   C   D   E

7   A   B   C   D   E

8   A   B   C   D   E

9   A   B   C   D   E

10   A   B   C   D   E

CONTINUE WORKING

Match the rotations shown in questions 11–15 to one of the original figures A, B, C, D or E.

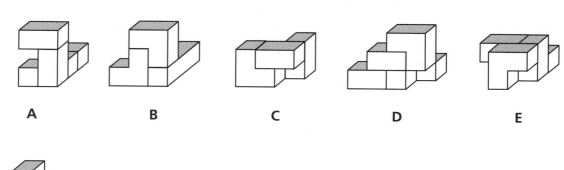

A   B   C   D   E

11

A   B   C   D   E

12

A   B   C   D   E

13

A   B   C   D   E

14

A   B   C   D   E

15

A   B   C   D   E

END OF PAPER

THIS PAGE HAS DELIBERATELY BEEN LEFT BLANK

Collins

Non-Verbal Reasoning Assessment Paper 6

Instructions:

1. Ensure you have pencils and an eraser with you.
2. Make sure you are able to see a clock or watch.
3. Write your name on the answer sheet.
4. Do not open the question booklet until you are told to do so by an adult.
5. Mark your answers on the answer sheet only.
6. All workings must be completed on a separate piece of paper.
7. You should not use a calculator, dictionary or thesaurus at any point in this paper.
8. Move through the sections as quickly as possible and with care.
9. Follow the instructions at the foot of each page.
10. You should mark your answers with a horizontal strike, as shown on the answer sheet.
11. If you want to change your answer, ensure that you rub out your first answer and that your second answer is clearly more visible.
12. You can go back and review any questions that are within the section you are working on only.

You should await further instructions before moving onto another section.

Symbols and Phrases used in the Tests

 Instructions

 Time allowed for this section

 Stop and wait for further instructions

 Continue working

SECTION 1: EXPLODED 3D FIGURES

INSTRUCTIONS

 YOU HAVE 8 MINUTES TO COMPLETE THE FOLLOWING SECTION.

YOU HAVE 15 QUESTIONS TO COMPLETE WITHIN THE TIME GIVEN.

Example i

Look at the figure on the left. Which group of blocks could be used to make the figure on the left?

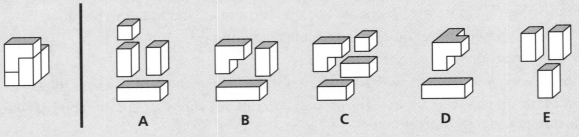

The correct answer is **C**. This has already been marked in Example i in Section 1 of your answer sheet on page 160.

Example ii

Look at the figure on the left. Which group of blocks could be used to make the figure on the left?

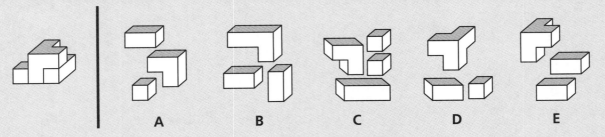

The correct answer is **D**. Mark the answer D in Example ii in Section 1 of your answer sheet on page 160.

STOP AND WAIT FOR FURTHER INSTRUCTIONS

In these questions, select the option (A, B, C, D or E) that shows the set of blocks that could be used to make the figure on the left.

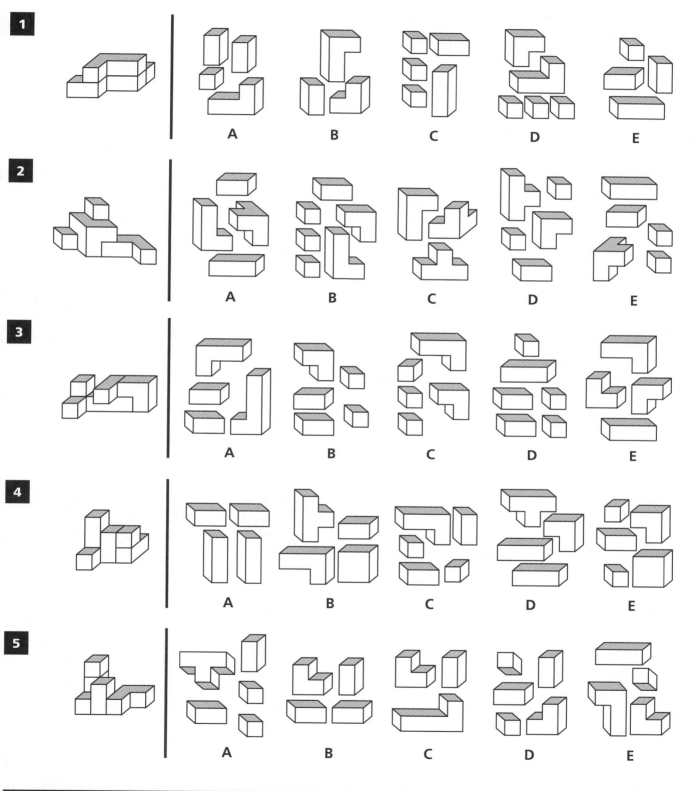

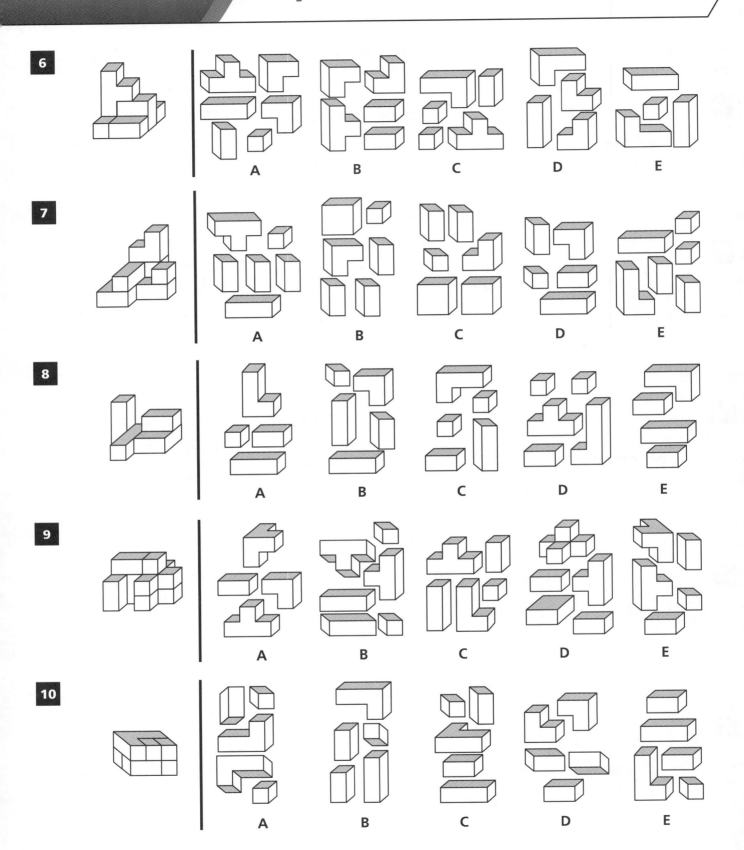

6　A　B　C　D　E

7　A　B　C　D　E

8　A　B　C　D　E

9　A　B　C　D　E

10　A　B　C　D　E

CONTINUE WORKING

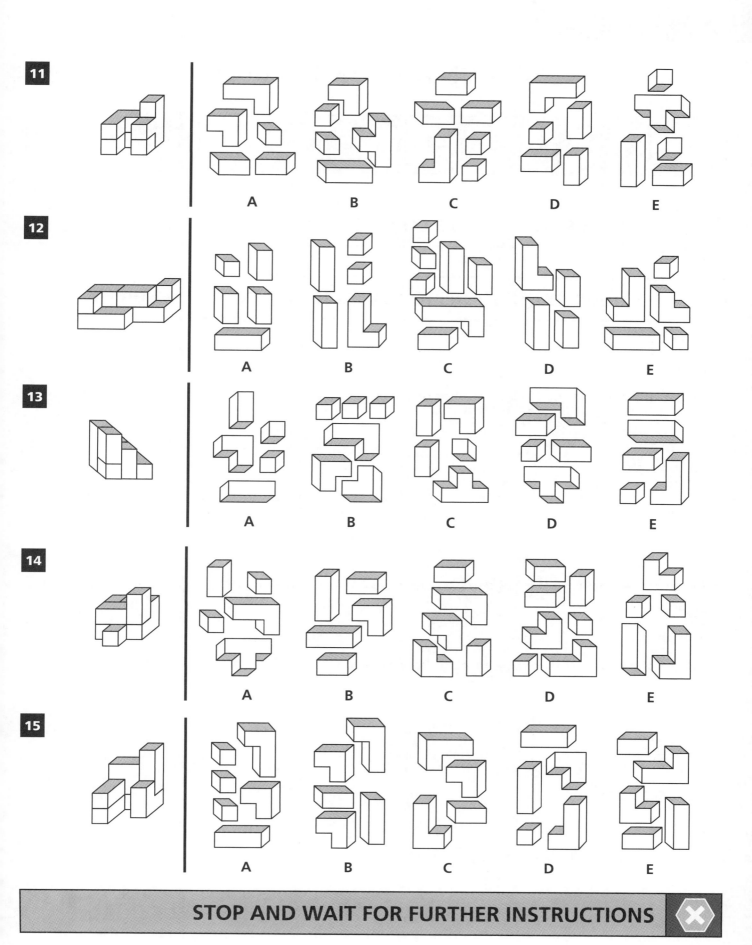

SECTION 2: FACES ON CUBES

 INSTRUCTIONS

 YOU HAVE 8 MINUTES TO COMPLETE THE FOLLOWING SECTION.

YOU HAVE 15 QUESTIONS TO COMPLETE WITHIN THE TIME GIVEN.

Example i

The net of a cube is shown. One face has been selected. Which face would be opposite the given face when the net is folded?

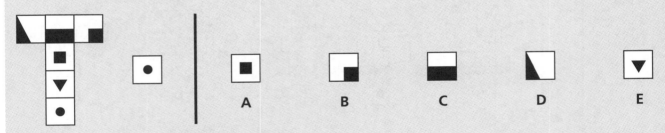

The correct answer is **A**. This has already been marked in Example i in Section 2 of your answer sheet on page 160.

Example ii

The net of a cube is shown. One face has been selected. Which face would be opposite the given face when the net is folded?

The correct answer is **D**. Mark the answer D in Example ii in Section 2 of your answer sheet on page 160.

STOP AND WAIT FOR FURTHER INSTRUCTIONS

In each of these questions, the net of a cube is shown and one face has been selected. Which face would be opposite the given face when the net is folded? Choose A, B, C, D or E.

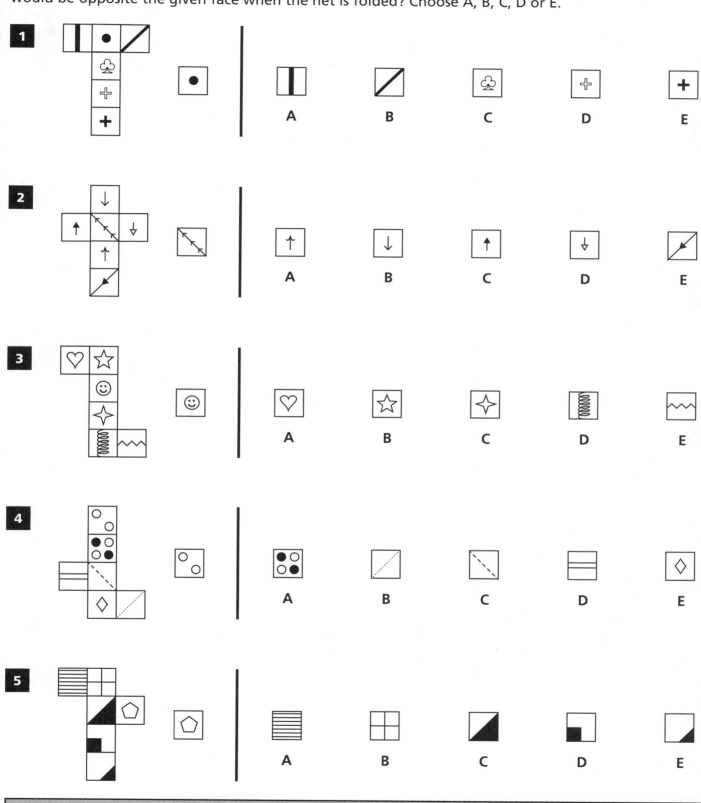

6 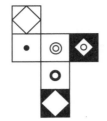 |

| | A | B | C | D | E |

7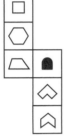

8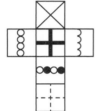

9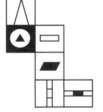

10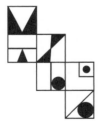

CONTINUE WORKING

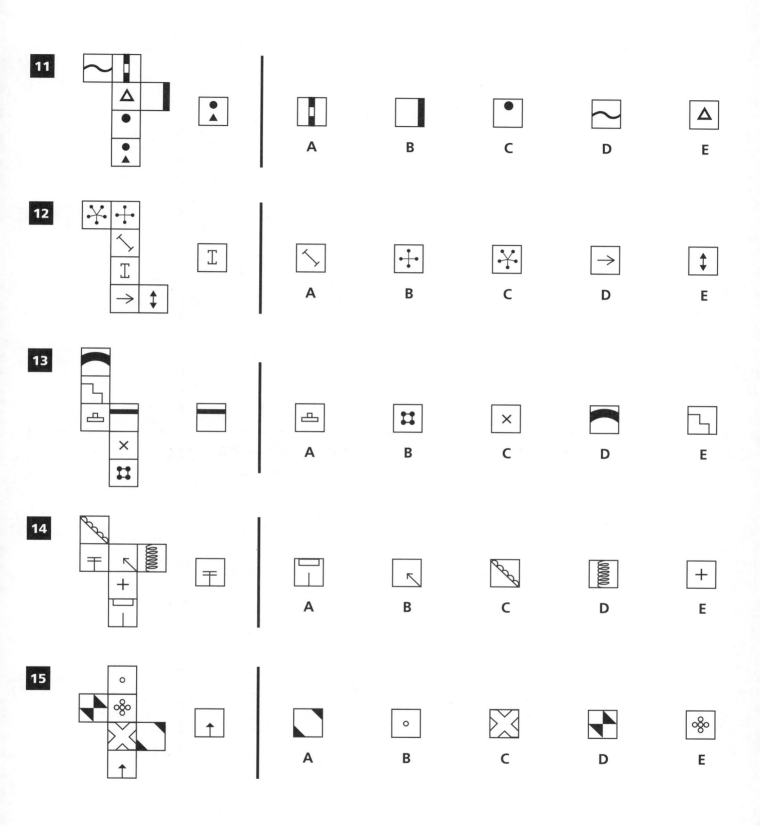

END OF PAPER

THIS PAGE HAS DELIBERATELY BEEN LEFT BLANK

Collins

11+
Non-Verbal Reasoning
Answers

For the CEM test

Pages 6–13: Making Connections
Page 10: Quick Test
1. a) **E**

   Triangle E is made up of dashed lines.The other triangles are made up of solid lines.

   b) **E**

   Shape E is a rectangle. The other shapes are all squares of different sizes.

2. a) **C**

   Arrow C matches the two arrows on the left because it has an identical arrowhead. All the other arrows have different styles of head to those on the left.

   b) **E**

   Triangle E matches the two triangles on the left because it is also an isosceles triangle.

Page 13: Quick Test
1. a) **C**

   Shape C matches the two shapes on the left because it is also a white square made up of solid lines.

   b) **A**

   Image A matches the two images on the left because it also has two dark green segments and two light green segments.

   c) **E**

   Image E matches the two images on the left because it also has an alternating pattern of small squares (green squares follow white squares and white squares follow green squares). The arrow is a distraction.

Pages 14–25: Finding Relationships
Page 20: Quick Test
1. a) **C**

   The images in the boxes swap sizes and positions. There are no changes to the shading and there is no rotation.

   b) **B**

   Squares become circles, circles become triangles and triangles become squares. Solid green shapes become white, white shapes become striped and striped shapes become solid green.

2. a) **B**

   The shapes in image B have a total of nine corners. This matches the number of corners in each of the two images on the left.

   b) **E**

   Image E also has three of its eight segments shaded in.

3. a) **E**

   The two small shapes move outside of the larger shape. The larger shape does not move.

   b) **B**

   The shaded shape slides up over the white shape until the patterns join together.

Page 25: Quick Test
1. a) **B**

   The first shape of each pair is reflected in a vertical mirror line.

   b) **C**

   In the first pair of images, the car body and roof change from white to solid shading and the whole image is reflected in a vertical mirror line. In image C both the body and sail of the boat have taken the solid shading and the whole image has been reflected in a vertical mirror line.

2. a) **E**

   The first image in each pair is reflected in a horizontal mirror line.

   b) **D**

   The first image in each pair is reflected in a diagonal mirror line going from the bottom left to the top right.

   c) **A**

   In the first image of each pair, the outer shading moves 90° clockwise while the inner shading moves 45° anti-clockwise.

Pages 26–36: Spotting Patterns
Page 30: Quick Test
1. **B**

   From left to right, the shape in each box gets smaller and the shading changes from solid green to white.

2. **B**

   The images in each box are reflected in a horizontal mirror line. The images in the bottom row of the grid are a reflection of the images in the top row.

3. **D**

   From left to right, the white images in the boxes pick up an alternating solid green and white shading pattern. In the right-hand column, the top segment of the outer layer is white and the segments then alternate between solid green and white. The top segment of the inner layer is solid green and the segments then alternate between white and solid green.

Page 36: Quick Test
1. **A**

   As the shapes in the boxes move down to the next row in each column, they get smaller. The shapes are reflected in a horizontal mirror line (or rotated 180°) as they move down a row.

2. **E**

   The top row contains three different images. As you go down to the next row, the images move one box along to the right. The images are also rotated 90° anti-clockwise.

3. **C**

   The first column of boxes is reflected in a vertical mirror line to make the last column of boxes and the shapes within them swap colours.

Pages 37–43: Completing Sequences
Page 40: Quick Test
1. **B**

   The triangle rotates 180° each time and alternates between green and white.

2. **D**

   One of the circles is removed and a triangle is added in each box as the pattern moves from left to right. All the shapes alternate between solid shading and white with each step.

3. **E**

   The shaded circle moves one place around the star each time in a clockwise direction, stopping between the points. The star doesn't move.

Page 43: Quick Test
1. **C**

   There are two patterns in this sequence. The first happens with every step – the image is reflected in a horizontal mirror line each time. The second happens with every other step – the shaded circle moves to the next point of the small shaded triangle in an anti-clockwise direction in every other box.

2. **D**

   The number of triangles increases by three in each box as the pattern moves from left to right.

3. **B**

   The number of circles decreases by two in each box as the pattern moves from left to right.

Pages 44–45: Breaking Codes
Page 45: Quick Test
1. a) **B**

   A, C and B are the codes for the shading. M, L and N are the codes for the number of small squares. The fifth shape is spotted (C) and has three small squares (M). The answer is CM.

   b) **D**

   D and E are the codes for the direction of the diagonal strip. H, I and J are the codes for the style of the top of the shield. X, Y and Z are the codes for the shading of the shield. The fifth shape has a diagonal strip that goes from top left to bottom right (E), the shield has three points at the top (I) and the shield is vertically striped (X). The answer is EIX.

Pages 46–48: Paper Folding and Identifying Shapes
Page 48: Quick Test
1. a) **B**

   The rectangle appears in option B.

   b) **D**

   The irregular hexagon appears in option D.

2. a) **E**

   When the paper is unfolded, the holes would appear as shown.

   b) **C**

   When the paper is unfolded, the holes would appear as shown.

3. D

By combining the three shapes on the left (and rotating two of them), you can create the figure shown in option D.

Pages 49–51: Nets of Cubes
Page 51: Quick Test
1. a) **A** and **B**
   b) They would not fold to make a cube as some of the faces would overlap, leaving gaps where no other faces were.
2. a) **D**
   The triangle shown on the cube does not appear on the net.
   b) **D**
   The short line shown on the cube would actually be the shaded circle.
3. a) **E**
   This is the only net that could make the given cube.
   b) **D**
   This is the only net that could make the given cube.

Pages 52–56: 3D Figures
Page 56: Quick Test
1. a) **D**
   b) **C**
2. a) **B**
   b) **A**
3. **C**
   Option C shows the blocks that could make the figure. The L-shaped block would be at the front, the cuboid at the back left and the cube at the back right.

Practice Answers

Pages 58–60
Practice Test 1: Making Connections
1. **E**
   All of the shapes have nine sides except for E, which has 11.
2. **A**
   All of the arrows point upwards except for A, which points downwards.
3. **D**
   All of the shapes have at least one line of symmetry except for D, which has no lines of symmetry.
4. **B**
   The circles all have one inner segment and one outer segment that is unshaded except for B.
5. **A**
   All of the shapes have straight line shading patterns except for shape A, which is solid grey. It is also the only shape that contains right angles.
6. **E**
   The figures on the left are all shaded black. Therefore, the answer is E.
7. **B**
   The figures on the left each have four sides and no curved corners. Therefore, the answer is B.
8. **A**
   The figures on the left are all stars with an even number of points. Therefore, the answer is A.

9. **A**
   The figures on the left each consist of an outer shape with a white heart shape inside. Therefore, the answer is A.
10. **E**
    The figures on the left each consist of two shapes. The external shape has one more side than the internal shape. Therefore, the answer is E.
11. **C**
    The group of shapes in each of the first three boxes have 11 straight sides in total. Box C is the only one to match this.
12. **D**
    The first two shapes are isosceles triangles. Box D is the only one with an isosceles triangle in it.
13. **A**
    All of the individual shapes in the first two boxes have vertical lines of symmetry. Box A is the only other box where both shapes also have a vertical line of symmetry.
14. **B**
    The images are made up of a square surrounded by isosceles triangles. The triangles are split into two segments which are separated by their shading pattern. As you go clockwise around the image, the first segment of each triangle is shaded to match the square. The second segment of each triangle has a different shading pattern to the first segment. All of the second segments match each other.
15. **D**
    The car headlights on the first three images are all white. Car D is the only answer that matches this. All of the other shading and the position of the steering wheel are distractions.
16. **E**
    The first two boxes contain shapes with lines that are a regular dashed pattern. Option E is the only shape with the same pattern.

Pages 61–63
Practice Test 2: Finding Relationships
1. **A**
   The shading of the figure changes from white to black. Therefore, the answer is A.
2. **C**
   The figure is reflected in a vertical mirror line. Therefore, the answer is C.
3. **A**
   The outline of the figure changes from dashed to solid. Therefore, the answer is A.
4. **D**
   The figure rotates 90° anti-clockwise and its shading changes from white to black. Therefore, the answer is D.
5. **C**
   The line shading of the figure changes to the opposite direction. Therefore, the answer is C.
6. **A**
   The shape in the top left-hand corner changes to match the size and shape of the bottom-right corner shape, although it retains its original shading

pattern. The larger of the two other shapes moves under the smaller one and they swap shading patterns. Therefore, the answer is A.
7. **C**
   The square changes into a star with the same number of points. The points of the star are along a line from the centre of the original square through the middle of each side. As the pentagon has a horizontal edge at the top, the five-pointed star must point straight up. Therefore, the answer is C.
8. **B**
   The image rotates 90° clockwise. The shading pattern on the middle segment swaps with the other segments. The angle of the pattern is rotated with the image. The thickness of the lines does not change. Therefore, the answer is B.
9. **D**
   The segments rotate and join together to form a larger shape. The segments stay in the same area of the box. Therefore, the answer is D.
10. **B**
    The segments fold out and the shading moves one segment clockwise. Therefore, the answer is B.
11. **E**
    The shapes are reflected in a vertical mirror line and the shapes in the bottom left and top right of the box swap shading styles. Therefore, the answer is E.
12. **D**
    The image is reflected in a vertical mirror line and the shading style of the shapes within it swaps with that of the background. Therefore, the answer is D.
13. **B**
    The shapes are reflected in a horizontal mirror line running through the middle of the box. The shading in the group of four shapes moves one shape to the right, while the shading in the group of three shapes moves one shape to the left. The shading patterns are not reflected. Therefore, the answer is B.
14. **E**
    The image is reflected in a horizontal mirror line. Therefore, the answer is E.
15. **C**
    The whole box is reflected in a horizontal mirror line. The shading pattern moves to the next shape in an anti-clockwise direction. Therefore, the answer is C.
16. **C**
    The box is reflected in a diagonal mirror line going from bottom left to top right. The segmented shape is a distraction as it doesn't look like it has been reflected at all, merely translated. Therefore, the answer is C.
17. **A**
    The box is reflected in a diagonal mirror line going from top left to bottom right. Therefore, the answer is A.
18. **D**
    The shading patterns on the outer segments of the image rotate 90°

clockwise while the shading patterns on the inner segments rotate 90° anti-clockwise. Therefore, the answer is D.

19. C
The shape rotates 90° anti-clockwise and the shading changes from black to white. Therefore, the answer is C.

Pages 64–66
Practice Test 3: Spotting Patterns

1. D
The line in the second column becomes a corner before it moves to the first column. The other shape is turned into a regular shape, keeping the same height as the original. There is still a gap between the shapes. Therefore, the answer is D.

2. C
The figure in the top right is the same as the figure in the top left except it is shaded black instead of white. Therefore, the figure in the bottom right should be the same as the figure in the bottom left except it should be shaded black. Therefore, the answer is C.

3. A
The figure in the top right is a reflection of the figure in the top left in a vertical mirror line. Therefore, the figure in the bottom right should be a reflection of the figure in the bottom left in a vertical mirror line. Therefore, the answer is A.

4. C
The figure in the top right has one more side than the figure in the top left. Both figures are shaded white. Therefore, the figure in the bottom right should have one more side than the figure in the bottom left. Both figures should be shaded white. Therefore, the answer is C.

5. C
The figure in the top right is the same as the figure in the top left except the line shading is in the opposite direction. Therefore, the figure in the bottom right should be the same as the figure in the bottom left except the line shading should be in the opposite direction.Therefore, the answer is C.

6. B
To get from the top row to the bottom row, the shapes are reflected in a horizontal mirror line and the shading changes. If it was white it becomes black, and if it was black it becomes white. Therefore, the answer is B.

7. C
The images in the first column are reflected in a vertical mirror line into the second column. Therefore, the answer is C.

8. A
All the segments of the star that were white in the first column are grey in the second column. The segments that were grey become black and the ones that were black become white. Therefore, the answer is A.

9. C
The image in the first column is taken apart in the second column. For the 'clock' image this means that the circle for the face, the hand section, the pendulum arm and the pendulum itself are all separated. Nothing is rotated. Therefore, the answer is C.

10. E
The grid has a vertical mirror line running down the middle of the second column. The first column is reflected in that line to become the third column and the shapes are shaded black. Therefore, the answer is E.

11. C
From one row to the one below, the shapes move one box to the right, but the shading patterns move one box to the left. All of the first row shapes are in the top left of their boxes, the second row shapes are in the middle of their boxes and the bottom row shapes are in the bottom right of their boxes. Therefore, the answer is C.

12. A
The shapes in each box work as one image. Each image moves down to the next row, moves one box to the left and rotates 90° clockwise. Therefore, the answer is A.

13. C
As the images move down a row, they rotate 45° clockwise and move one box to the left. Therefore, the answer is C.

14. A
The first column has small white shapes in the top left corner of the boxes. The last column has large black shapes in the bottom right corner of the boxes. The middle column contains an image in the centre of the box made up of the white shape in the middle of the black shape. The images rotate 90° clockwise from one column to the next. Therefore, the answer is A.

Pages 67–69
Practice Test 4: Completing Sequences

1. C
The shapes in the box alternate between a striped circle and a grey oval. The missing shape is a grey oval. Therefore, the answer is C.

2. D
The shapes are symmetrical in a vertical mirror line that goes through the third box, so the shapes in the second and fourth boxes are identical and the shapes in the first and last box should be identical. The missing shape is a grey square. Therefore, the answer is D.

3. A
The boxes alternate between grey and black circular shapes. Therefore, the answer is A.

4. B
From left to right, each box has one fewer black shape in it. Therefore, the correct answer box should have two black shapes in it. Therefore, the answer is B.

5. B
From left to right, the heart shape rotates 90° clockwise from one box to the next. Therefore, the answer is B.

6. B
From left to right, the pentagon moves in a clockwise direction from one corner to the next. From left to right, the circle does likewise. Therefore, the answer is B.

7. C
From left to right, each shape has one more side than the shape in the preceding box. Therefore, the correct answer box contains a shape with seven sides. Therefore, the answer is C.

8. D
The shapes all look like regular shapes that have been squashed horizontally. Going from left to right, the shapes lose one side in each box. The missing shape is a tall pentagon. The shading is a distraction. Therefore, the answer is D.

9. B
The shading pattern inside the diamond rotates 45° anti-clockwise in each box from left to right. The missing shape is a diamond with vertically striped shading. The arrows are a distraction. Therefore, the answer is B.

10. A
From left to right, two squares are removed from each box and an octagon is added at the top. The squares are removed from the top, working from left to right on each row. Therefore, the answer is A.

11. C
The triangle is reflected in a horizontal mirror line in each box. Whenever it points upwards it has white shading; when it points down it has black shading. The pentagon is reflected in a horizontal mirror line in every second box, with the direction of the stripes reflecting as well. Therefore, the answer is C.

12. E
The shading pattern of the inner segments rotates one segment clockwise while the shading of the outer segments rotates one segment anti-clockwise. The outer shape switches between being a circle and a square. Therefore, the answer is E.

13. D
The boxes alternate between a growing square pattern and a repeating circle pattern. The circles rotate around the box in an anti-clockwise direction, while the squares go in a clockwise direction. Therefore, the answer is D.

14. C
Moving left to right, the squares move from the bottom to the top of each box and back again. The black square moves one along to the right. The circles do not move but the grey shading moves one circle clockwise while the black shading moves two circles anti-clockwise. When the same circle should have both types of shading, only the black is seen. Therefore, the answer is C.

15. A

Moving left to right, one circle becomes a triangle. The triangle closest to the edge of the box changes its shading between white and black each time and the other triangles alternate along the line. The whole shape rotates 90° anti-clockwise from one box to the next. Therefore, the answer is A.

16. B

Moving left to right, the number of shapes in each box decreases by three each time. The shapes alternate between four- and five-pointed stars. Therefore, the answer is B.

17. D

Moving left to right, the number of shapes in each box is two more than the last. The specific shapes are distractions. Therefore, the answer is D.

18. B

The boxes have the sequence of square numbers in them with 25 shapes in the first box, 16 in the second and so on. There should be 9 shapes in the empty box. The shading of all the shapes inside any box should be the same. The specific shapes are distractions. Therefore, the answer is B.

19. E

The boxes alternate between having triangles and squares in them. The number of shapes is the sequence of triangular numbers so the fourth box should have 10 squares in it. Neither squares nor triangles rotate, which excludes option B. The shading patterns are a distraction. Therefore, the answer is E.

Pages 70–71
Practice Test 5: Breaking Codes

1. A

A, B and C are the codes for which point of the star is shaded – top, bottom left or bottom right. N, O and P are the codes for the shading – solid black, grey or striped. The bottom-right point on the fifth star is shaded (C) and the shading is grey (O). The answer is CO.

2. A

The first letter is for the type of star: D – four-pointed; F – five-pointed; E – six-pointed. The second letter is for the shading pattern: S – vertical stripes; T – horizontal stripes; R – white. The orientation of the stars and patterns around their edges are distractions. The fifth shape is a five-pointed star (F) and white (R). The answer is FR.

3. D

The images all look like the front of a car. The first letter is for the side the steering wheel is on: P – the steering wheel is on the left; Q – the steering wheel is on the right; R – the steering wheel is not visible. The second letter is for the body shading (but not the roof): T – white; S – black; U – grey. The shading of the windscreen banner and the roof are distractions. The steering

wheel on the fifth image is on the right (Q) and the car has a white body (T). The answer is QT.

4. C

The first letter is for the shape of the top of the shield: G – double curve; E – straight; F – single curve. The second letter describes the number of shapes on the shield: K – two shapes; J – three shapes; L – four shapes. The shading on the shields is a distraction. The fifth shape has a single curve on the shield (F) and has three shapes inside it (J). The answer is FJ.

5. C

The first letter is for the tail of the arrow: E – one fin; D – no fins; F – two fins. The second letter describes the head of the arrow: P – diamond head; Q – round head; O – triangular head. The orientation of the arrows is a distraction. The fifth shape has two fins (F) and a diamond head (P). The answer is FP.

6. E

The first letter is for the combination of shapes: V – circle and pentagon; U – square and triangle; W – circle and triangle. The second letter is for the shading: A – vertical stripes; C – horizontal stripes; B – grey. The position of the shapes is a distraction. The fifth image has a square and triangle (U) and is grey (B). The answer is UB.

7. C

The first letter is for the shading of the centre of the image: C – black; A – grey; B – white. The second letter is for the orientation: E – vertical/horizontal; F – diagonal. The third letter is for the shading of the triangles: I – white; J – grey; H – black. The fifth shape has a grey centre (A), has a diagonal orientation (F) and the triangles are shaded black (H). The answer is AFH.

8. B

The first letter is for the shading of the second half of each triangle as you go in a clockwise direction around the image: O – black; Q – striped; P – white. The second letter is for the shading at the centre of the image: R – striped; T – black; S – white. The third letter is for the shading of the first half of each triangle as you go in a clockwise direction around the image: W – white; U – grey; V – black. The fifth image has the second half of each triangle shaded black (O), the centre of the image is black (T) and the first half of the triangle is black (V). The answer is OTV.

9. A

The first letter is the shading on the top triangle of the star: V – striped; W – spotted; U – black. The second letter is for a vertical line of symmetry: O – there is a vertical line of symmetry; P – there is no vertical line of symmetry. The third letter is for the shading on the lowest two triangles: D – grey; B – striped; C – white. The shading of the pentagon in the middle and the higher two triangles are distractions. The fifth shape has a black

triangle at the top (U), a vertical line of symmetry (O) and the lower triangles are grey (D). The answer is UOD.

10. B

The first letter is for the middle block of each image: E – no shading; F – striped; G – grey. The second letter is for the bottom block: L – black; M – striped; K – grey. The third letter is for the top block: S – striped; U – black; T – grey. The fifth shape has a striped middle block (F), a grey bottom block (K) and a grey top block (T). The answer is FKT.

11. E

The first letter describes whether the arrow is pointing up or down: B – down; A – up. The second letter is for the style of the arrowhead: C – triangular head; D – diamond head; E – round head. The third letter describes whether the arrow is pointing left or right: G – left; F – right. The fifth shape is pointing down (B), has a round arrowhead (E) and is pointing to the left (G). The answer is BEG.

12. E

The first letter is for the basic shape: N – triangle; M – quadrilateral; O – pentagon. The second letter is for whether or not the shape is regular: C – irregular; B – regular. The third letter is for the shading of the shape: Y – grey; Z – black; X – striped. The fifth shape is a pentagon (O), is irregular (C) and is shaded black (Z). The answer is OCZ.

13. B

The images all look like houses. The first letter is for whether or not the house has a chimney: F – it has a chimney; G – it does not have a chimney. The second letter is for the number of floors: L – one floor; M – two floors; K – three floors. The third letter is for the shading of the roof: U – white; V – striped; T – black. The fifth shape has a chimney (F), two floors (M) and a black roof (T). The answer is FMT.

14. E

The images all look like a boat at sea. The first letter is for the wave style: B – the waves are pointed; D – there are no waves; C – the waves are curved. The second letter is for the sail: I – the sail is pointing to the right; H – the sail is pointing to the left. The third letter is for the colour of the hull of the boat: V – black; W – striped; X – grey. The fifth shape has no waves (D), a sail pointing to the left (H) and a grey hull (X). The answer is DHX.

Pages 72–73
Practice Test 6: Paper Folding and Identifying Shapes

1. E

When the paper is unfolded, the holes would appear as shown.

2. D

When the paper is unfolded, the holes would appear as shown.

3. D

When the paper is unfolded, the holes would appear as shown.

4. C
When the paper is unfolded, the holes would appear as shown.

5. E
When the paper is unfolded, the holes would appear as shown.

6. D
When the paper is unfolded, the holes would appear as shown.

7. C
The right-angled triangle appears in option C.

8. A
The irregular hexagon appears in option A.

9. C
The isosceles triangle appears in option C.

10. B
The irregular quadrilateral appears in option B.

11. B
The circle appears in option B.

Pages 74–75
Practice Test 7: Nets of Cubes

1. D
When the net is folded, the oval will touch the two triangles as shown. You can eliminate option A as there is no small black square on the net; option B because the black squares on the front face appear in the opposite positions to what they would be; option C because the oval and the black circle have swapped places compared to where they would be when the net was folded; option E because the two large black triangles would be opposite one another when the net was folded.

2. C
When the net is folded, the two lines with dots would be positioned as shown and the double line would run vertically on the right-hand face. You can eliminate option A because it shows a horizontal, not diagonal, line with white circles; option B because it shows an unhappy face, not a smiling one; option D because it shows two lines with black dots; option E because it shows a black diamond, not a white one.

3. A
When the net is folded, the three faces will touch as shown. You can eliminate option B because the black and the white flat-ended lollipops have their bases touching rather than being parallel with one another; option C because the black and the white circles are in the wrong position; option D because the multiplication signs and one of the black and white circle patterns are opposite each other when the net is folded; option E because the plus signs and the white flat-ended lollipop appear on the wrong faces if the net is folded as shown.

4. D
When the net is folded, the faces can touch one another as shown. You can

eliminate option A because it has two fine plus signs; option B because the two chunky plus signs would appear swapped round if the cube were folded as shown; option C because the two chunky multiplication signs are opposite one another when the net is folded; option E because the bold black plus sign and the fine plus sign are opposite one another when the net is folded.

5. E
When the net is folded, the faces can touch as shown. You can eliminate options A and B because the right-hand face would be diagonal stripes, not solid black; option C because the triangles do not appear on the net; option D because the diagonal striped squares will be folded into the cube so that the shaded quarters do not touch directly, but instead they touch the white quarters.

6. E
When the net is folded, the spring and the white circle will be opposite each other. The cross and the black circle will be opposite each other; the horizontal line and the dashed diagonal line will be opposite each other.

7. B
When the net is folded, the black rectangle and the large cross will be opposite each other; the small cross and the triangles will be opposite each other; the arrow and the square will be opposite each other.

8. A
When the net is folded, the heart and the circles will be opposite each other; the star and the square will be opposite each other; the two triangles will be opposite the circle and triangle.

9. E
When the net is folded, the circle and the dot will be opposite the vertical striped shading; the empty circle will be opposite the diagonal striped shading; the black dot will be opposite the triangle.

10. C
When the net is folded, the striped quarters will be opposite the white circle; the black quarters will be opposite the black rectangle; the white rectangle will be opposite the black dot.

Pages 76–78
Practice Test 8: 3D Figures

1. A
2. D
3. B
4. A
5. C
6. A
   The rectangular blocks would be arranged on the left-hand side of the figure (two vertical and one horizontal) and the single cube would be arranged to the right-hand side of the figure. The two vertical blocks would be positioned next to each other at the back of the shape; the horizontal cuboid would be in front of them on the left-hand side.

7. B
The three-cube rectangular block would be arranged on the right-hand side of the figure, with one single cube sitting behind it on the far right-hand side and the other single cube sitting next to it on the left-hand side. The two two-cube rectangle blocks would be positioned horizontally on the left-hand side of the figure.

8. E
The L-shaped block would be positioned on the right-hand side of the figure, with the rectangular blocks positioned vertically and horizontally in the centre. The single cube would be to the left-hand side of the figure.

9. B
The three-cube cuboid block would sit at the back left of the figure. Two shorter cuboid blocks would sit horizontally in front and on top of it. One shorter cuboid block would sit horizontally at the right-hand side of the figure. The single cubes would sit at the front and top right-hand side of the figure.

10. C
The L-shaped block would be positioned upright on the right-hand side of the figure, with two single cubes in the middle row and the two cuboids positioned at the front and front left-hand side of the figure.

11. C
12. A
13. A
14. B
15. B

ASSESSMENT PAPER 1
Pages 80–83
Section 1: Views of 3D Figures

1. A
When viewed from above, the figure shows one cube aligned left in each of the front and second rows, followed by three cubes in each of the third and fourth rows.

2. D
When viewed from above, the figure shows two cubes in the front row with a space between them, followed by two rows of three cubes.

3. E
When viewed from above, the figure shows three cubes in the front row, a second row with no cubes, then a third row with three cubes.

4. E
When viewed from above, the figure shows two cubes in the front row aligned to the left, a second row with one cube aligned to the left, then a third row and fourth row each with two cubes (one aligned left and one aligned right with a space between them).

5. A
When viewed from above, the figure shows one cube in the front row aligned to the left, a second row with

144   11+ Non-Verbal Reasoning

two cubes aligned to the left, then a third row and fourth row each with three cubes.

6. **B**
When viewed from above, the figure shows two cubes in each of the front and second rows, and one cube in each of the third and fourth rows. The third and fourth rows are aligned to the right-hand side of the front rows.

7. **B**
When viewed from above, the figure has three cubes in the front row, three cubes in the middle row (aligned two to the left-hand side of the front row, one overhanging, and one to the right-hand side, attached by the corner) and one cube in the back row.

8. **C**
When viewed from above, the figure has five cubes in a single row.

9. **A**
When viewed from above, the figure has two cubes in the front row, three cubes in the middle row and one cube in the back row. The front row is aligned to the left-hand side of the middle row, and the back row is aligned to the right-hand side of the middle row.

10. **D**
When viewed from above, the figure has three cubes in the front row, separated into a single cube on the left-hand side and two cubes on the right-hand side. It has four cubes in the back row.

11. **D**
When viewed from above, the figure has four cubes in the front row, three cubes in the middle row and three cubes in the back row. The middle and back rows are aligned with the right-hand side of the front row.

12. **B**
When viewed from above, the figure has four cubes in the front row, three cubes in the second row and one cube in the third row. You can eliminate option D as there is no fourth cube in the second row on the left-hand side.

13. **B**
When viewed from above, the figure has four cubes in the front row and three cubes in the back row. The back row has two cubes to the left-hand side of the front row, overhanging by one cube, and one cube to the right-hand side.

14. **A**
When viewed from above, the figure has one cube in the front row, four cubes in the second row, one cube in the third row and one cube in the fourth row. The front row is aligned with the second cube from the left of the second row and the third and fourth rows are aligned with the right-hand side of the second row.

15. **C**
When viewed from above, the figure has three cubes in the front row and

two cubes in the back row, aligned with the left-hand side and centre of the front row.

Pages 84–87
Section 2: Complete the Grid

1. **E**
The figure in the top right rearranges the order and number of symbols in the figure in the top left. Therefore, the figure in the bottom right should rearrange the symbols in the figure in the bottom left in the same way. Therefore, the answer is E.

2. **D**
The figure in the top left consists of two triangles. In the figure in the top right, the external triangle rotates 90° clockwise and the internal triangle rotates 180°. Therefore, the figure in the bottom right should consist of the shapes in the figure in the bottom left rotated in the same way. Therefore, the answer is D.

3. **B**
From left to right in each row, the number of sides of each shape decreases by one. Therefore, the answer is B.

4. **C**
The third figure in each row consists of the first two figures laid one upon the other without rotation. Therefore, the answer is C.

5. **E**
From left to right in the first two rows, the arrow moves anti-clockwise around the corners of the boxes and rotates 90° anti-clockwise as it does so. At the same time, one of the two white shapes moves one position to the right and the shaded shape moves diagonally from the bottom right corner of the box to the top left. Applying the same changes to the last box of the third row means that E is the correct answer.

6. **B**
In the second and third rows, the larger shape rotates 90° clockwise as it moves clockwise around the sides of the box and increases in number by one in each column from left to right. The smaller shape moves clockwise by half the length of a side in each column. Applying the same changes to the first row means that B is the correct answer.

7. **B**
In the first row, the shape is reflected in a vertical line and any solid outlines become dashed (and vice-versa) in the next column. Applying the same changes to the second row means that B is the correct answer.

8. **C**
In the first and second rows, there is one box with two shapes, another box with four shapes and a third box with six shapes. In each box, half of the shapes are white and half are black. The third row already has boxes of two and of six diamonds, so the empty box will have four diamonds with two shaded black and two white. Therefore, C is the correct answer.

9. **D**
The corner boxes of the grid have a striped pattern, with the stripes building up from 1–4 in the same way as the concentric circles build up from 1–4 in the centrally positioned, outer boxes. Three stripes are therefore needed in the empty box. The stripes are always positioned diagonally across the corner of the box nearest the centre of the grid, so D is the correct answer.

10. **D**
From left to right in the first and third rows, the direction of the arrow moves anti-clockwise around the corners of the box. The arrow style remains the same across the row, so the empty box requires a black-headed arrow pointing to the bottom left corner. The two white shapes in the corners alternate from one side of the box to the other, with the upper one increasing in size from left to right. Therefore, D is the correct answer.

11. **B**
From the top row downwards, the shapes move one column to the right and reduce in size, but do not rotate. Therefore, B is the correct answer.

12. **D**
In each of the given boxes, the circle rotates 90° clockwise as it moves clockwise around the corners of the box from left to right. The other shaded (or patterned) shape interchanges between opposite corners from left to right across the columns. The answer is D because the half-shaded circle and the triangle with the dot are in the correct corners and the circle has been correctly rotated.

13. **C**
The two grey shields in the second column follow the movement and the shading change that occurs to the two white triangles (which move down the box and change to black) in the first column. The white single shield reverses its direction, enlarges and changes shading in the same way as the single black triangle in the top row of the first column. Therefore, the answer is C.

14. **A**
The first and third rows indicate that the middle column should be occupied by a large black shape and a separate, smaller white shape. Therefore, the answer is A.

15. **B**
The number of shapes in each box increases by one from left to right through the columns, with one of these shapes shaded black and any additional shapes in white. Looking down the columns, the black shape appears to be in a consistent position (in an upper position in the first column, in a central position in the second column and in a lower position in the third column). You can therefore expect the empty box to have three shapes, one of which will be black and positioned at the bottom of the box. The empty box can also be expected to have a small triangle at the

top left corner, in the same way that each row has one box with a circle at the top right. Therefore, the answer is B.

ASSESSMENT PAPER 2
Pages 90–93
Section 1: Complete the Sequence

1. **C**
   From left to right, the shape in each box rotates 45° anti-clockwise. Therefore, the answer is C.

2. **A**
   From left to right, each box contains a shape with one more side than in the preceding box. Therefore, the answer is A.

3. **A**
   From left to right, each box contains a black circle that moves two sides across on the shape in a clockwise direction. Therefore, the answer is A.

4. **E**
   From left to right, a quarter of a circle is added each time to the existing shape in each box. Therefore, the missing box should contain a full circle in the top right. Therefore, the answer is E.

5. **B**
   From left to right, the line shading of the shape in each box rotates 45° anti-clockwise. Therefore, the correct answer is B.

6. **B**
   At each step, from left to right, the shapes in the top-left corner gradually increase in size. At the same time, an extra 'diameter' line is added to the circle and an extra side is added to the shape around it. The answer is B (as opposed to A) because the circle has the additional line in the correct place for the sequence.

7. **E**
   At each step, from left to right, the arc rotates 90° clockwise around the square and the inner segment rotates 135° clockwise. Therefore, E is correct.

8. **C**
   At each step, from left to right, a square is added at the top-left corner of the box and any existing squares move from side to side and gradually towards the centre of the box. At each step, a circle is introduced from the bottom-right corner of the box and any existing circles then move from side to side and gradually towards the centre of the box. Therefore, the correct answer is C.

9. **C**
   The first, third and fifth boxes follow one sequence while the second and fourth boxes follow another. The answer is C because the opposite segment to that seen in the third box should be shaded black.

10. **D**
    At each step, from left to right, the the larger 'V' moves 90° anti-clockwise around the black diamond, while a smaller 'V' appears every other box. The two semi-circles move clockwise around the sides of the box. The zig-zag line increases in length as it moves anti-clockwise around the box. Therefore, D is correct.

11. **E**
    At each step, from left to right, the black circles increase in number by one and the point from which they start moves one place clockwise around the edge of the box. At the same time, the rectangle moves down the centre of the box and the direction of its shading alternates. Therefore, the correct answer is E.

12. **E**
    At each step, from left to right, the central circle alternates between black and white, while two 'petals' are lost. As shown by the third and fourth boxes, the petals are lost in an anti-clockwise direction from the top, hence the correct answer is E rather than D.

13. **D**
    At each step, from left to right, an extra circle is added inside a shape. The shape's number of sides reduces by one at each step, so the missing box will consist of a quadrilateral enclosing four circles. Therefore, the correct answer is D.

14. **C**
    At each step, from left to right, the striped pattern moves in a clockwise direction around the corner triangles of the box while the white circle moves in an anti-clockwise direction. The white triangle and black shading also move around the inner triangles in opposite directions to each other. Therefore, the correct answer is C.

15. **D**
    At each step, from left to right, the small white square moves from the bottom left corner to the top left corner and back again. The curved shape moves anti-clockwise around the corners of the box, while the diagonal line moves clockwise around the corners. The three black circles stay in fixed positions. Therefore, the correct answer is D.

Pages 94–97
Section 2: Connections

1. **A**
   The second figure is a 45° clockwise rotation of the first figure. So the answer is a 45° clockwise rotation of the third figure, the answer is A.

2. **C**
   The second figure consists of two reflected versions of the shape in the first figure with stripes that go from top left to bottom right in the upper shape and bottom left to top right for the lower shape. Therefore, the answer must have the same striped pattern as in the second figure. Therefore, the answer is C.

3. **E**
   The shape in the second figure has one fewer side and contains one fewer circle than the shape in the first figure. The same changes must be made to the third figure. Therefore, the answer is E.

4. **C**
   The right half of the shape in the first figure is removed in the second figure. Therefore, the right half of the shape in the third figure must also be removed. Therefore, the answer is C.

5. **A**
   The shapes in the first figure are rearranged to form the second figure. The shapes in the third figure must be rearranged in the same way. Therefore, the answer is A.

6. **C**
   In the first pair, the two diamonds inside the circle become two circles inside a diamond in the right-hand image. At the same time, the outline used for a circle changes from dashed to a heavy, solid style. In the second pair, you can expect the changes to occur in reverse, since the starting image consists of a large triangle with a solid outline enclosing two squares with heavy, solid outlines. Therefore, C is the correct answer.

7. **D**
   In the first pair, the left-hand image rotates 90° clockwise to produce the right-hand image. Making the same change for the second pair means that D is the correct answer.

8. **B**
   In the first pair, the left-hand image rotates 90° clockwise to produce the right-hand image. The diamond is duplicated so that it 'slots' into either side of the larger shape and the shapes swap shading. Making the same changes for the second pair means that B is the correct answer.

9. **E**
   In the first pair, the left-hand image rotates 90° anti-clockwise to produce the right-hand image. The two smaller shapes are also reflected to opposite sides of the larger shape. Making these changes for the second pair means that E is the correct answer.

10. **A**
    In the first pair, the shapes in the left-hand image change size and position to produce the right-hand image. The outer hexagon reduces in size and encloses the circle, which moves from the upper left to the centre of the image. The square becomes the largest, outer shape and it rotates 45° as it does so. Making the same changes for the second pair means that A is the correct answer.

11. **E**
    In the first pair, the left-hand image rotates 180° and changes from black to white to produce the right-hand image. Making these changes in reverse for the second pair means that E is the correct answer.

12. **A**
    In the first pair, the pair of semi-circles in the left-hand image become triangles in the right-hand image but the longer straight edge of the inner black shape swaps sides. Making the same changes for the second pair (this time using two pairs of semi-circles but with the inner ones reversed in orientation compared with the outer ones) means that A is the correct answer.

13. **D**
    In the first pair, the pieces of the left-hand image come apart and rotate approximately 45° anti-clockwise to

produce the right-hand image. Making the same changes for the second pair means that D is the correct answer.

14. **A**

In the first pair, the left-hand image rotates 150° anti-clockwise to produce the right-hand image. Making the same change for the second pair means that A is the correct answer.

15. **E**

In the first pair, the triangle in the left-hand image enlarges and moves so that it overlaps the right-hand side of the circle. The triangle is then reflected in a vertical line so that it also overlaps the left-hand side of the circle in the second image. Making the same changes for the second pair means that E is the correct answer.

ASSESSMENT PAPER 3
Pages 100–103
Section 1: Least Similar

1. **D**

All the other figures are rotations of the same shape.

2. **A**

In all the other figures, the black shape is at the back.

3. **E**

All the other figures consist of the same five shapes.

4. **E**

All the other figures have more lines on the top than on the bottom and all the other figures have an odd number of lines.

5. **E**

In all the other figures, from the top row downwards, the number of triangles stays the same or decreases.

6. **D**

In all the other images the black dot is positioned in the smaller of the overlapping shapes.

7. **E**

In all the other images the arrow is pointing away from the black square.

8. **D**

The answer is D because the arrow in the central shape is pointing away from the straight-ended side unlike the other images.

9. **C**

All the other images have pentagons, rather than a quadrilateral, with dots at each corner.

10. **B**

In all the other images the two angles are marked by one curved arc in combination with one 'squared' arc. B is the only image in which the angles are marked by two 'squared' arcs.

11. **D**

In all the other images the opposite-facing circular shapes have a matching pattern. In option D, one of the pairs of circular shapes does not have a matching pattern.

12. **D**

In all the other images the outer black circle is positioned on the other side of the figure, relative to the white circle.

13. **C**

In all the other images the black arcs on the circles on the upper triangle are aligned towards the black arcs that are in the corners of the lower triangle. In option C, two of the black arcs on the upper triangle are not aligned to the black arcs on the lower triangle.

14. **A**

A is the only image where the two shapes could be rotated to fit exactly one over the other.

15. **B**

In image B, the white circle is placed to the other side of the black segment compared with the other options.

Pages 104–107
Section 2: Nets of Cubes

1. **D**

When the net is folded, the black triangle on the front face will touch the cross which forms the upper face of the cube. The black rectangle will be at the back of the right-hand face. You can eliminate option A as the black rectangle does not touch the cross with a long side; option B because the cross and the triangle are on the wrong faces; option C as the small cross does not appear on the net; and option E as the two crosses are opposite one another when the net is folded.

2. **A**

When the net is folded with the concentric circles on the top face, the small white circle will be on the front and the small black circle on the right-hand face as shown. You can eliminate option B as the large and concentric circles are opposite one another when the net is folded; option C as the large black circle is not shown on the net; option D as the small black circle and the smiley face will be opposite one another; and option E because the large white circle and the concentric circles are opposite one another.

3. **A**

When the net is folded with the stripes on the front face as shown, the black diamond is on the top face and the small white circle on the right-hand face. You can eliminate option B because the black square does not appear on the net; option C because the rectangle and the small circle are opposite when the net is folded; option D because the stripes and the small black circle with the diagonal line are opposite when the net is folded; and option E because the single black circle does not appear on the net.

4. **E**

When the net is folded with the small black triangles as shown on the cube in E, the black lemon shapes will be on the top face. You can eliminate option A because the black lemon shapes and the bold stripe would be opposite one another when the net is folded; option B because the white lemon shapes and the black triangle will be opposite one

another; option C because the white lemons and the dashed line would be perpendicular to one another rather than parallel; and option D because the bold line would be pointing towards the black triangle.

5. **B**

When the net is folded with the two triangles as shown on the front face, the circles would be on the top face and the black rectangle on the right-hand side. You can eliminate option A as the black rectangle and the black square will be opposite each other when the net is folded; option C as the black rectangle will touch the stripes along one of the rectangle's shorter sides; option D as the square and the rectangle will be opposite one another when the net is folded; option E as the stripes and the circles will be opposite one another when the net is folded.

6. **B**

When the net is folded with the triangle on the front face as shown, the black scallops will be on the top face and the white scallops on the right-hand face. You can eliminate option A because the two black and white squared faces have alternating black and white sections, not touching; option C because the black scallops point away from the black triangle; option D because the white triangle points towards the black scallops; and option E because the black and white squares are in the opposite places to how they are shown on the net.

7. **E**

When the net is folded with the long line horizontal on the front face, the short line will be on the top face and the white-headed arrow will point down on the right-hand face. You can eliminate option A as the black-headed arrow and the fine arrow do not point at one another; option B because there are not two white-headed arrows; option C because the white-headed arrow would point down rather than up; and option D because the short single line and the black-headed arrow are opposite one another.

8. **C**

When the net is folded with the four-pointed black star on the front face, the black heart will be on the top face and the white heart on the right-hand face as shown. You can eliminate options A and D because the black heart and the black five-pointed star are opposite when the net is folded; option B because the four-pointed stars are opposite one another when the net is folded; and option E because the hearts should point at one another.

9. **E**

When the net is folded, the parallel lines will touch the short black lines and the rectangle as shown in E. You can eliminate option A as the parallel lines are shown in the opposite direction to how they would be if the cube was folded; option B because the four-pointed star does not appear on the net; option C because the rectangle would be on the left-hand face, not the right-hand face; and option D because the oval and the star have been swapped compared to how they would actually be when the net is folded.

10. A

When the net is folded as shown in A, the irregular pentagon would be on the front face pointing towards the regular hexagon on the right-hand face and the black shield would be on the top face, pointing left. You can eliminate option B because the arrowhead would be on the bottom face (hidden) if the cube was positioned as shown; option C because there is not a regular white pentagon on the net; option D because the white shield and the black shield are not pointing towards each other; and option E because the white shield would not point to the curved part of the black shield.

11. A

When the net is folded as shown in A, the bold arrowhead will point to the square, with the bold cross to the right-hand side. You can eliminate option B because the bold line and the fine arrowhead have swapped places compared to how they would be if the net was folded; options C and D because the bold arrowhead points away from the bold line; and option E because the dashed line would originate from the corner between the square and the fine arrowhead, not the opposite corner as shown.

12. D

When the net is folded as shown in D, the black equilateral triangle points to the large white equilateral triangle. You can eliminate option A because the black triangle points to the black circle, not the large white equilateral triangle; option B because the concentric triangle should be parallel with the side that joins the black circle; option C because the black triangle is not pointing to the large white equilateral triangle; and option E because the black isosceles triangle would be on the left-hand face (hidden).

13. C

When the net is folded, the smiley face and the diagonal-striped shaded face will be opposite one another, not next to one another.

14. B

When the net is folded, the black square shown on the cube would not be in that position (the four small circles would be) and the stepped line would not touch the large cross in that way.

15. C

When the net is folded, the diagonal lines and the small squares would be as shown in answer option B, rather than as shown in answer option C.

ASSESSMENT PAPER 4
Pages 110–113
Section 1: Rotation

1. C
   All of the other options are reflections or different shapes from the original figure.
2. B
   All of the other options are different shapes from the original figure.
3. E
   All of the other options are reflections or different shapes from the original figure.
4. D
   All of the other options are different shapes from the original figure.
5. E
   All of the other options are different shapes from the original figure.
6. A
   All of the other options are different shapes from the original figure.
7. A
   All of the other options are different shapes from the original figure.
8. D
   All of the other options are different shapes from the original figure.
9. E
   All of the other options are different shapes from the original figure.
10. E
    All of the other options are different shapes from the original figure.
11. C
    All of the other options are different shapes from the original figure.
12. C
    All of the other options are different shapes from the original figure.
13. B
    All of the other options are different shapes from the original figure.
14. D
    All of the other options are different shapes from the original figure.
15. A
    All of the other options are different shapes from the original figure.

Pages 114–117
Section 2: Reflection

1. E
2. D
3. B
4. C
5. C
6. A
7. D
8. E
9. B
10. E
11. D
12. C
13. B
14. A
15. A

ASSESSMENT PAPER 5
Pages 120–123
Section 1: Most Similar

1. A
   The three figures on the left are all fractions equivalent to one half. Therefore, the answer is A.
2. E
   The three figures on the left each consist of a black line that crosses over a shape at one point only. Therefore, the answer is E.
3. E
   The three figures on the left each have no lines of symmetry. Therefore, the answer is E.
4. A
   The three figures on the left are all rotations of the same shape. Therefore, the answer is A.
5. C
   The three figures on the left all contain a square border with grey line shading in the same direction. Therefore, the answer is C.
6. C
   The three figures on the left are all three-quarters of a whole shape. Therefore, the answer is C.
7. D
   In each figure on the left, the square on the left contains more black circles than the square on the right. Therefore, the answer is D.
8. A
   The three figures on the left all have a vertical line of symmetry. Therefore, the answer is A.
9. D
   The three figures on the left all have an hour hand pointing at an even number. Therefore, the answer is D.
10. E
    The three figures on the left each consist of four arrows that rotate 45° from left to right in a clockwise direction. Therefore, the answer is E.
11. C
    The figures on the left-hand side all show arrows turning clockwise.
12. D
    The figures on the left are all made up of smaller shapes. The bottom right-hand small shape is shaded black and positioned at the front of the group.
13. C
    The figures on the left-hand side all have a total of 12 sides.
14. C
    The figures on the left-hand side are all composed of a square which has one-quarter striped. The bottom left-hand side of the square also has a shaded black corner in the shape of a triangle.
15. D
    The figures on the left-hand side are all composed of an arrow in a rectangle, with an arrowhead at one side and a perpendicular line or lines at the other, the style of which exactly matches the arrowhead.

Section 2: Rotated 3D Figures
1. B
2. D
3. A
4. E
5. C
6. A
7. E
8. B
9. C
10. D
11. D
12. B
13. A
14. E
15. C

ASSESSMENT PAPER 6
Pages 130–133
Section 1: Exploded 3D Figures
1. A

The L-shaped block would sit at the top, with the two cuboids beneath. The single cube would sit at the back.

2. A

The corner block would sit at the front; the L-shaped block would sit at the right-hand side; the longer cuboid would sit at the back of the shape horizontally; the shorter cuboid would be positioned vertically, sticking up.

3. E

The cuboid would be positioned horizontally, with the two short L-shaped blocks positioned at either end and the longer L-shaped block overhanging in the middle.

4. C

The L-shaped block would be on the left-hand side of the figure, with the two cuboids positioned vertically and horizontally at the middle and right-hand side respectively. One single cube would be positioned behind the middle cuboid, and the other on top of the right-hand cuboid.

5. D

The L-shaped block would be on the right-hand side of the figure, with the two cuboids positioned vertically in the middle and left-hand side of the figure. The single cubes would be on the left-hand side of the figure.

6. B

The T-shaped block is positioned upright on the left-hand side of the figure, resting on a cuboid. The two L-shaped blocks are interlinked on the right-hand side of the figure, with the second cuboid behind. It cannot be option A as there are too many pieces to link together to make the figure shown.

7. C

One large square cuboid would be positioned at the front left-hand side of the figure, with a smaller cuboid on top. The other square cuboid would be positioned on a short end, supporting the L-shaped block at the back. The second small cuboid would be positioned on the right-hand side of the figure with the single cube on top.

8. B

The two long cuboids would be positioned on the left-hand side of the figure; the L-shaped block and the single cube would be on the bottom right-hand side of the figure. The short cuboid would be positioned on top of the right-hand side of the figure.

9. D

The corner block would be positioned at the top right-hand side of the figure, with the T-shaped block below; the three cuboids would be positioned to the left-hand side of the figure.

10. A

The L-shaped blocks would be positioned at the back of the figure; the cuboid would be at the bottom to the front left-hand side; the two single cubes would be at the front top right-hand side.

11. B

The T-shaped block would be positioned upright on the right-hand side of the figure, with a single cube underneath it at the front and another directly to the left of it. The L-shaped block would be above this second single cube to the left-hand side. The long cuboid would extend to the back of the figure on the left-hand side.

12. C

The L-shaped block would be at the bottom right-hand side of the figure with a single cube to its left; the long cuboid would be at the front left with a single cube on top of the cuboid and on top of the L-shaped block. The two short cuboids would be on the top.

13. C

The T-shaped block would be positioned vertically at the back of the figure on the left-hand side; the L-shaped block would tuck underneath it. One cuboid would be positioned on top of the single cube at the front left-hand side of the figure; the other would be positioned horizontally on the right-hand side.

14. C

The long L-shaped block would be placed in the centre of the figure with the two short L-shaped blocks either side of it. The cuboids would be positioned horizontally and vertically at the front of the figure.

15. B

The long L-shaped block would be on the left-hand side of the figure at the bottom; the short cuboid would be above it to the front left-hand side of the figure. The short L-shaped blocks would be in the middle of the figure and on the front right-hand side of the figure. The long cuboid would be positioned vertically to the back right-hand side of the figure.

Pages 134–137
Section 2: Faces on Cubes
1. D

When the net is folded, the circle will be opposite the white cross. The club will be opposite the black cross. The diagonal and vertical lines will be opposite one another.

2. E

When the net is folded, the three arrows will be opposite the bold diagonal arrowhead. The fine arrow and the twisted arrow will be opposite each other. The bold black arrow and the white arrow will be opposite one another.

3. D

When the net is folded, the smiley face will be opposite the spring. The two stars will be opposite each other, and the heart will be opposite the zigzag.

4. C

When the net is folded, the two circles will be opposite the dashed line. The four circles will be opposite the diamond, and the parallel lines will be opposite the dotted line.

5. A

When the net is folded, the pentagon will be opposite the horizontal striped shading. The quartered face will be opposite the small square, and the large and the small triangles will be opposite one another.

6. C

When the net is folded, the white square with a white background will be opposite the bold circle. The small black dot will be opposite the small white dot inside a square with a black background. The concentric circles will be opposite the white square with a black background.

7. D

When the net is folded, the regular hexagon will be opposite the irregular hexagon shown in option D. The square and the trapezium will be opposite each other. The curved black shape will be opposite the irregular hexagon shown in option E.

8. B

When the net is folded, the scallops will be opposite the white circles. The multiplication sign will be opposite the black and white circles, and the bold cross and the dashed cross will be opposite each other.

9. A

When the net is folded, the parallelogram will be opposite the large white triangle. The small black triangle in a circle will be opposite the small rectangles which have one shaded black. The white rectangle will be opposite the small white rectangles.

10. E

When the net is folded, the two scalene triangles will be opposite the large black circle and triangle. The two right-angled triangles will be opposite the black circle and the rectangle shown in option A. The small black triangle and rectangle in option C will be opposite the small square and dot shown in option B.

11. **E**

When the net is folded, the bold triangle will be opposite the circle and triangle. The wave will be opposite the thin black rectangle. The dot will be opposite the three rectangles which have two shaded black.

12. **B**

When the net is folded, the ornate capital I will be opposite the four dots. The plainer capital I will be opposite the single-ended arrow. The double-ended arrow and the five dots will be opposite each other.

13. **B**

When the net is folded, the black rectangle will be opposite the square with dots at each corner. The curve and the face which shows a square and rectangle will be opposite each other. The step and the cross will be opposite each other.

14. **D**

When the net is folded, the spring and the two short lines intersected by another line will be opposite one another. The diagonal scalloped line and the cross will be opposite each other. The arrow and the rectangle with a short line will be opposite each other.

15. **E**

When the net is folded, the arrow and the four circles will be opposite each another. The hourglass and the small black triangles will be opposite each another. The small circle and the four white triangles will be opposite each another.

THIS PAGE HAS DELIBERATELY BEEN LEFT BLANK

Progress Charts

Track your progress by shading in your score at each attempt.

Assessment Papers

	Score	Date:	Attempt 1	Paper 1: Section 1
/15	Score	Date:	Attempt 2	
/15	Score	Date:	Attempt 1	Paper 1: Section 2
/15	Score	Date:	Attempt 2	
/15	Score	Date:	Attempt 1	Paper 2: Section 1
/15	Score	Date:	Attempt 2	
/15	Score	Date:	Attempt 1	Paper 2: Section 2
/15	Score	Date:	Attempt 2	
/15	Score	Date:	Attempt 1	Paper 3: Section 1
/15	Score	Date:	Attempt 2	
/15	Score	Date:	Attempt 1	Paper 3: Section 2
/15	Score	Date:	Attempt 2	
/15	Score	Date:	Attempt 1	Paper 4: Section 1
/15	Score	Date:	Attempt 2	
/15	Score	Date:	Attempt 1	Paper 4: Section 2
/15	Score	Date:	Attempt 2	
/15	Score	Date:	Attempt 1	Paper 5: Section 1
/15	Score	Date:	Attempt 2	
/15	Score	Date:	Attempt 1	Paper 5: Section 2
/15	Score	Date:	Attempt 2	
/15	Score	Date:	Attempt 1	Paper 6: Section 1
/15	Score	Date:	Attempt 2	
/15	Score	Date:	Attempt 1	Paper 6: Section 2
/15	Score	Date:	Attempt 2	

Practice Tests

	Score	Date:	Attempt 1	Practice Test 1: Making Connections
/16	Score	Date:	Attempt 2	
/16	Score	Date:	Attempt 1	Practice Test 2: Finding Relationships
/19	Score	Date:	Attempt 2	
/19	Score	Date:	Attempt 1	Practice Test 3: Spotting Patterns
/14	Score	Date:	Attempt 2	
/14	Score	Date:	Attempt 1	Practice Test 4: Completing Sequences
/19	Score	Date:	Attempt 2	
/19	Score	Date:	Attempt 1	Practice Test 5: Breaking Codes
/14	Score	Date:	Attempt 2	
/14	Score	Date:	Attempt 1	Practice Test 6: Paper Folding and Identifying Shapes
/11	Score	Date:	Attempt 2	
/11	Score	Date:	Attempt 1	Practice Test 7: Nets of Cubes
/10	Score	Date:	Attempt 2	
/10	Score	Date:	Attempt 1	Practice Test 8: 3D Figures
/15	Score	Date:	Attempt 2	

Practice Test 1: Making Connections

Example i

	A	B	C	D	E
1	A	B	C	D	E
2	A	B	C	D	E
3	A	B	C	D	E
4	A	B	C	D	E
5	A	B	C	D	E

Example ii

	A	B	C	D	E
6	A	B	C	D	E
7	A	B	C	D	E
8	A	B	C	D	E
9	A	B	C	D	E
10	A	B	C	D	E
11	A	B	C	D	E
12	A	B	C	D	E
13	A	B	C	D	E
14	A	B	C	D	E
15	A	B	C	D	E
16	A	B	C	D	E

Practice Test 2: Finding Relationships

Example

	A	B	C	D	E
1	A	B	C	D	
2	A	B	C	D	
3	A	B	C	D	
4	A	B	C	D	
5	A	B	C	D	
6	A	B	C	D	E
7	A	B	C	D	E
8	A	B	C	D	E
9	A	B	C	D	E
10	A	B	C	D	E
11	A	B	C	D	E
12	A	B	C	D	E
13	A	B	C	D	E
14	A	B	C	D	E
15	A	B	C	D	E
16	A	B	C	D	E
17	A	B	C	D	E
18	A	B	C	D	E
19	A	B	C	D	E

Practice Test 3: Spotting Patterns

Example

	A	B	C	D	E
1	A	B	C	D	E
2	A	B	C	D	E
3	A	B	C	D	E
4	A	B	C	D	E
5	A	B	C	D	E
6	A	B	C	D	E
7	A	B	C	D	E
8	A	B	C	D	E
9	A	B	C	D	E
10	A	B	C	D	E
11	A	B	C	D	E
12	A	B	C	D	E
13	A	B	C	D	E
14	A	B	C	D	E

Practice Test 4: Completing Sequences

Example

	A	B	C	D	E
1	A	B	C	D	E
2	A	B	C	D	E
3	A	B	C	D	E
4	A	B	C	D	E
5	A	B	C	D	E
6	A	B	C	D	E
7	A	B	C	D	E
8	A	B	C	D	E
9	A	B	C	D	E
10	A	B	C	D	E
11	A	B	C	D	E
12	A	B	C	D	E
13	A	B	C	D	E
14	A	B	C	D	E
15	A	B	C	D	E
16	A	B	C	D	E
17	A	B	C	D	E
18	A	B	C	D	E
19	A	B	C	D	E

Practice Test 5: Breaking Codes
Example

	A	B	C	D	E
	A	■	C	D	E
1	A	B	C	D	E
2	A	B	C	D	E
3	A	B	C	D	E
4	A	B	C	D	E
5	A	B	C	D	E
6	A	B	C	D	E
7	A	B	C	D	E
8	A	B	C	D	E
9	A	B	C	D	E
10	A	B	C	D	E
11	A	B	C	D	E
12	A	B	C	D	E
13	A	B	C	D	E
14	A	B	C	D	E

Practice Test 7: Nets of Cubes
Example i

	A	B	C	D	E
	A	B	■	D	E
1	A	B	C	D	E
2	A	B	C	D	E
3	A	B	C	D	E
4	A	B	C	D	E
5	A	B	C	D	E

Example ii

	A	B	C	D	E
	A	■	C	D	E
6	A	B	C	D	E
7	A	B	C	D	E
8	A	B	C	D	E
9	A	B	C	D	E
10	A	B	C	D	E

Practice Test 6: Paper Folding and Identifying Shapes
Example i

	A	B	C	D	E
	★	B	C	D	E
1	A	B	C	D	E
2	A	B	C	D	E
3	A	B	C	D	E
4	A	B	C	D	E
5	A	B	C	D	E
6	A	B	C	D	E

Example ii

	A	B	C	D	E
	A	B	C	■	E
7	A	B	C	D	E
8	A	B	C	D	E
9	A	B	C	D	E
10	A	B	C	D	E
11	A	B	C	D	E

Practice Test 8: 3D Figures
Example i

	A	B	C	D
	A	B	■	D
1	A	B	C	D
2	A	B	C	D
3	A	B	C	D
4	A	B	C	D
5	A	B	C	D

Example ii

	A	B	C	D	E
	A	B	C	■	E
6	A	B	C	D	E
7	A	B	C	D	E
8	A	B	C	D	E
9	A	B	C	D	E
10	A	B	C	D	E

Example iii

	A	B	C
	A	■	C
11	A	B	C
12	A	B	C
13	A	B	C
14	A	B	C
15	A	B	C

Pupil's Full Name:

Instructions:
Mark the boxes correctly like this ✦

Please sign your name here:

Section 1: Views of 3D Figures
Example i

Ⓐ   Ⓑ   ⬤   Ⓓ   Ⓔ

Example ii

Ⓐ   Ⓑ   Ⓒ   Ⓓ   Ⓔ

1   Ⓐ   Ⓑ   Ⓒ   Ⓓ   Ⓔ

2   Ⓐ   Ⓑ   Ⓒ   Ⓓ   Ⓔ

3   Ⓐ   Ⓑ   Ⓒ   Ⓓ   Ⓔ

4   Ⓐ   Ⓑ   Ⓒ   Ⓓ   Ⓔ

5   Ⓐ   Ⓑ   Ⓒ   Ⓓ   Ⓔ

6   Ⓐ   Ⓑ   Ⓒ   Ⓓ   Ⓔ

7   Ⓐ   Ⓑ   Ⓒ   Ⓓ   Ⓔ

8   Ⓐ   Ⓑ   Ⓒ   Ⓓ   Ⓔ

9   Ⓐ   Ⓑ   Ⓒ   Ⓓ   Ⓔ

10   Ⓐ   Ⓑ   Ⓒ   Ⓓ   Ⓔ

11   Ⓐ   Ⓑ   Ⓒ   Ⓓ   Ⓔ

12   Ⓐ   Ⓑ   Ⓒ   Ⓓ   Ⓔ

13   Ⓐ   Ⓑ   Ⓒ   Ⓓ   Ⓔ

14   Ⓐ   Ⓑ   Ⓒ   Ⓓ   Ⓔ

15   Ⓐ   Ⓑ   Ⓒ   Ⓓ   Ⓔ

Section 2: Complete the Grid
Example i

Ⓐ   Ⓑ   Ⓒ   ⬤   Ⓔ

Example ii

Ⓐ   Ⓑ   Ⓒ   Ⓓ   Ⓔ

1   Ⓐ   Ⓑ   Ⓒ   Ⓓ   Ⓔ

2   Ⓐ   Ⓑ   Ⓒ   Ⓓ   Ⓔ

3   Ⓐ   Ⓑ   Ⓒ   Ⓓ   Ⓔ

4   Ⓐ   Ⓑ   Ⓒ   Ⓓ   Ⓔ

5   Ⓐ   Ⓑ   Ⓒ   Ⓓ   Ⓔ

6   Ⓐ   Ⓑ   Ⓒ   Ⓓ   Ⓔ

7   Ⓐ   Ⓑ   Ⓒ   Ⓓ   Ⓔ

8   Ⓐ   Ⓑ   Ⓒ   Ⓓ   Ⓔ

9   Ⓐ   Ⓑ   Ⓒ   Ⓓ   Ⓔ

10   Ⓐ   Ⓑ   Ⓒ   Ⓓ   Ⓔ

11   Ⓐ   Ⓑ   Ⓒ   Ⓓ   Ⓔ

12   Ⓐ   Ⓑ   Ⓒ   Ⓓ   Ⓔ

13   Ⓐ   Ⓑ   Ⓒ   Ⓓ   Ⓔ

14   Ⓐ   Ⓑ   Ⓒ   Ⓓ   Ⓔ

15   Ⓐ   Ⓑ   Ⓒ   Ⓓ   Ⓔ

Pupil's Full Name:

Instructions:
Mark the boxes correctly like this ✦

Please sign your name here:

2

Section 1: Complete the Sequence
Example i

	A	B	C	D	E

Example ii

	A	B	C	D	E

	A	B	C	D	E
1	A	B	C	D	E
2	A	B	C	D	E
3	A	B	C	D	E
4	A	B	C	D	E
5	A	B	C	D	E
6	A	B	C	D	E
7	A	B	C	D	E
8	A	B	C	D	E
9	A	B	C	D	E
10	A	B	C	D	E
11	A	B	C	D	E
12	A	B	C	D	E
13	A	B	C	D	E
14	A	B	C	D	E
15	A	B	C	D	E

Section 2: Connections
Example i

	A	B	C	D	E

Example ii

	A	B	C	D	E

	A	B	C	D	E
1	A	B	C	D	E
2	A	B	C	D	E
3	A	B	C	D	E
4	A	B	C	D	E
5	A	B	C	D	E
6	A	B	C	D	E
7	A	B	C	D	E
8	A	B	C	D	E
9	A	B	C	D	E
10	A	B	C	D	E
11	A	B	C	D	E
12	A	B	C	D	E
13	A	B	C	D	E
14	A	B	C	D	E
15	A	B	C	D	E

Pupil's Full Name:

3

Instructions:
Mark the boxes correctly like this ✈

Please sign your name here:

Section 1: Least Similar
Example i

| | A | B | C | D | E |

Example ii

| | A | B | C | D | E |

	A	B	C	D	E
1	A	B	C	D	E
2	A	B	C	D	E
3	A	B	C	D	E
4	A	B	C	D	E
5	A	B	C	D	E
6	A	B	C	D	E
7	A	B	C	D	E
8	A	B	C	D	E
9	A	B	C	D	E
10	A	B	C	D	E
11	A	B	C	D	E
12	A	B	C	D	E
13	A	B	C	D	E
14	A	B	C	D	E
15	A	B	C	D	E

Section 2: Nets of Cubes
Example i

| | A | B | C | D | E |

Example ii

| | A | B | C | D | E |

	A	B	C	D	E
1	A	B	C	D	E
2	A	B	C	D	E
3	A	B	C	D	E
4	A	B	C	D	E
5	A	B	C	D	E
6	A	B	C	D	E
7	A	B	C	D	E
8	A	B	C	D	E
9	A	B	C	D	E
10	A	B	C	D	E
11	A	B	C	D	E
12	A	B	C	D	E
13	A	B	C	D	E
14	A	B	C	D	E
15	A	B	C	D	E

Pupil's Full Name:

4

Instructions:
Mark the boxes correctly like this ★

Please sign your name here:

Section 1: Rotation

Example i

	A	B	C	D	E

Example ii

	A	B	C	D	E

	A	B	C	D	E
1	A	B	C	D	E
2	A	B	C	D	E
3	A	B	C	D	E
4	A	B	C	D	E
5	A	B	C	D	E
6	A	B	C	D	E
7	A	B	C	D	E
8	A	B	C	D	E
9	A	B	C	D	E
10	A	B	C	D	E
11	A	B	C	D	E
12	A	B	C	D	E
13	A	B	C	D	E
14	A	B	C	D	E
15	A	B	C	D	E

Section 2: Reflection

Example i

	A	B	C	D	E

Example ii

	A	B	C	D	E

	A	B	C	D	E
1	A	B	C	D	E
2	A	B	C	D	E
3	A	B	C	D	E
4	A	B	C	D	E
5	A	B	C	D	E
6	A	B	C	D	E
7	A	B	C	D	E
8	A	B	C	D	E
9	A	B	C	D	E
10	A	B	C	D	E
11	A	B	C	D	E
12	A	B	C	D	E
13	A	B	C	D	E
14	A	B	C	D	E
15	A	B	C	D	E

Pupil's Full Name:

Instructions:
Mark the boxes correctly like this ✦

Please sign your name here:

Section 1: Most Similar

Example i

	A	B	C	D	E

Example ii

	A	B	C	D	E

	A	B	C	D	E
1	A	B	C	D	E
2	A	B	C	D	E
3	A	B	C	D	E
4	A	B	C	D	E
5	A	B	C	D	E
6	A	B	C	D	E
7	A	B	C	D	E
8	A	B	C	D	E
9	A	B	C	D	E
10	A	B	C	D	E
11	A	B	C	D	E
12	A	B	C	D	E
13	A	B	C	D	E
14	A	B	C	D	E
15	A	B	C	D	E

Section 2: Rotated 3D Figures

Example i

	A	B

Example ii

	A	B

	A	B	C	D	E
1	A	B	C	D	E
2	A	B	C	D	E
3	A	B	C	D	E
4	A	B	C	D	E
5	A	B	C	D	E
6	A	B	C	D	E
7	A	B	C	D	E
8	A	B	C	D	E
9	A	B	C	D	E
10	A	B	C	D	E
11	A	B	C	D	E
12	A	B	C	D	E
13	A	B	C	D	E
14	A	B	C	D	E
15	A	B	C	D	E

Pupil's Full Name:

Instructions:
Mark the boxes correctly like this ✦

Please sign your name here:

Section 1: Exploded 3D Figures
Example i

	Ⓐ	Ⓑ	⬤	Ⓓ	Ⓔ

Example ii

	Ⓐ	Ⓑ	Ⓒ	Ⓓ	Ⓔ

1	Ⓐ	Ⓑ	Ⓒ	Ⓓ	Ⓔ
2	Ⓐ	Ⓑ	Ⓒ	Ⓓ	Ⓔ
3	Ⓐ	Ⓑ	Ⓒ	Ⓓ	Ⓔ
4	Ⓐ	Ⓑ	Ⓒ	Ⓓ	Ⓔ
5	Ⓐ	Ⓑ	Ⓒ	Ⓓ	Ⓔ
6	Ⓐ	Ⓑ	Ⓒ	Ⓓ	Ⓔ
7	Ⓐ	Ⓑ	Ⓒ	Ⓓ	Ⓔ
8	Ⓐ	Ⓑ	Ⓒ	Ⓓ	Ⓔ
9	Ⓐ	Ⓑ	Ⓒ	Ⓓ	Ⓔ
10	Ⓐ	Ⓑ	Ⓒ	Ⓓ	Ⓔ
11	Ⓐ	Ⓑ	Ⓒ	Ⓓ	Ⓔ
12	Ⓐ	Ⓑ	Ⓒ	Ⓓ	Ⓔ
13	Ⓐ	Ⓑ	Ⓒ	Ⓓ	Ⓔ
14	Ⓐ	Ⓑ	Ⓒ	Ⓓ	Ⓔ
15	Ⓐ	Ⓑ	Ⓒ	Ⓓ	Ⓔ

Section 2: Faces on Cubes
Example i

	✦	Ⓑ	Ⓒ	Ⓓ	Ⓔ

Example ii

	Ⓐ	Ⓑ	Ⓒ	Ⓓ	Ⓔ

1	Ⓐ	Ⓑ	Ⓒ	Ⓓ	Ⓔ
2	Ⓐ	Ⓑ	Ⓒ	Ⓓ	Ⓔ
3	Ⓐ	Ⓑ	Ⓒ	Ⓓ	Ⓔ
4	Ⓐ	Ⓑ	Ⓒ	Ⓓ	Ⓔ
5	Ⓐ	Ⓑ	Ⓒ	Ⓓ	Ⓔ
6	Ⓐ	Ⓑ	Ⓒ	Ⓓ	Ⓔ
7	Ⓐ	Ⓑ	Ⓒ	Ⓓ	Ⓔ
8	Ⓐ	Ⓑ	Ⓒ	Ⓓ	Ⓔ
9	Ⓐ	Ⓑ	Ⓒ	Ⓓ	Ⓔ
10	Ⓐ	Ⓑ	Ⓒ	Ⓓ	Ⓔ
11	Ⓐ	Ⓑ	Ⓒ	Ⓓ	Ⓔ
12	Ⓐ	Ⓑ	Ⓒ	Ⓓ	Ⓔ
13	Ⓐ	Ⓑ	Ⓒ	Ⓓ	Ⓔ
14	Ⓐ	Ⓑ	Ⓒ	Ⓓ	Ⓔ
15	Ⓐ	Ⓑ	Ⓒ	Ⓓ	Ⓔ